MR. CITIZEN

By Harry S. Truman

YEAR OF DECISIONS
YEARS OF TRIAL AND HOPE

MR. CITIZEN

Harry S. Truman

PUBLISHED BY
BERNARD GEIS ASSOCIATES
DISTRIBUTED BY RANDOM HOUSE

Library of Congress Catalog Card Number 60-10127

Designed by Edwin H. Kaplin

Manufactured in the United States of America by American Book-Stratford Press, New York

To All Peoples Who Cherish Freedom

ACKNOWLEDGMENTS

I am very grateful to Mrs. Truman for the help and encouragement she gave in the reading and correction of the manuscript of this book. Her suggestions and corrections were invaluable.

And I express my gratitude to William Hillman and David M. Noyes, my friends and advisers, for their collaboration in the preparation of this book.

H.S.T.

Preface

How does it feel to give up the power and the great heights of the Presidency and once again be just a plain citizen?

This is one of the questions most persistently asked me by people curious about what goes on in the mind of a man who, in a matter of a few minutes, moves from the spotlight at the center of the world's greatest power to retirement and designed obscurity. In the time that it takes for the Chief Justice of the United States, on Inaugural Day, to administer the oath of office to the new President, a transfer of power takes place that is unparalleled in all history.

Whatever my personal feelings were at the moment I ceased to be President, the thought that was foremost in my mind was how orderly and simple was the transference of this great power vested by the people in their Chief Executive. This event, which takes place every four years except when a President dies in office, reaffirms the soundness and reality of our great Republic.

But as I was leaving the Inaugural platform, I wondered what other Presidents must have thought as they were stepping down into an unknown future. Long before I had even the remotest notion that I would become President, I had felt that the nation was wasteful in not making use of the unique experience of our Chief Executives who survived their term of office, sound of mind and body.

One of the reasons why I have written this book is to point out this long neglect in not making available to our country the counsel and knowledge of former Presidents. And I hope that our lawmakers can be persuaded to find a statutory way to make use of them in some appropriate capacity. For our history shows that an incumbent President may not always feel free to call on a former President.

I have put off publication of this book for seven years because I did not want it to be self-serving. In those years I have had an opportunity to record something of what happened to one former President after his return to private life.

Since I am given to plain speaking, especially on matters where I feel it necessary to point up an issue, there are some passages in this book that may be interpreted as harsh to certain individuals. But nothing I have written here is intended to be unfriendly to anyone.

H.S.T.

Contents

MR. CITIZEN

1

From 'Mr. President' to 'Mr. Citizen'

IT was January 20, 1953, when it became my time to take part in the ceremonies of turning the office of the Presidency over to Dwight D. Eisenhower. Washington, on that day, was cold and clear but not uncomfortable. The President-elect and I were sitting in the room of the sergeant-at-arms in the Capitol, waiting to go out through the Rotunda to the Inaugural platform.

Suddenly General Eisenhower turned to me and said: "I wonder who is responsible for my son John being ordered to Washington from Korea? I wonder who is trying to embarrass me?"

I answered: "The President of the United States ordered your son to attend your Inauguration. The President thought it was right and proper for your son to witness the swearing-in of his father to the Presidency. If you think somebody was trying to embarrass you by this order then the President assumes full responsibility."

I thought this was a curious reaction by a father to the presence of his son on an occasion so historic for himself and his family. I could only account for it on the grounds that this was a manifestation of hostility towards me.

At this moment, the sergeant-at-arms indicated it was time for us to go out to the platform. Ten minutes later, Dwight D. Eisenhower, standing on the Inaugural platform before Chief Justice Fred M. Vinson, took the oath of office as our new President and commander-in-chief, so swift and complete was the shift of authority and responsibility.

And so ended my authority over Major John Eisenhower and all other authority as well.

I TRIED to listen attentively to Eisenhower's Inaugural Address. But I was preoccupied with many thoughts. My principal concern, on turning over the Presidency, was how our foreign affairs would be conducted by the new Administration to guard the peace of the world. How would it deal with the Communist challenge to the free world? How would it get along with our allies? But the responsibility of government was no longer mine. What I had to think about now was what I was going to do. One thing was certain: I wanted to go home as quickly as possible. When President Eisenhower finished his Inaugural Address, Mrs. Truman, Margaret and I left the crowded scene at the Capitol.

Events and duties of office had been so pressing up to the last hour of my Administration that I could give little consideration to what was ahead of me. When a man serves his term in a place of importance, he ought to be willing to step aside while he is yet able to continue and let the next man take charge. The tragedy of too many men in public office has been that they did not know when to quit. This was one of the reasons why I had not sought another term in 1952 although I could have done so, since under the new constitutional amendment limiting the President to two terms in office, I was specifically excluded from its restrictions. In our democracy, we must constantly make room for new men to rise and to take over responsibilities, to assure that we do not lose the continuity of the government and the momentum of our growth and development.

And yet, it was not possible for me suddenly to break off my concern with what was going on in the world. It had been my lot to be identified not only with the major events of a decade but also with decisions that might well influence the future course of civilization. At no time had I presumed to possess a special gift of omniscience in dealing with what we had to face. I never felt that I was in any sense the indispensable man, and I hope that this nation will never believe in the notion of an indispensable man.

I had some misgivings as to where the new Administration might take us. Despite the falsehoods and distortions of the election campaign, I hoped that the Administration would continue the basic policies established by previous administrations that were essential and vital to our future. Although the responsibility was no longer mine, how could I detach myself from events with which I had been so intimately associated for so long? The truth is that it was impossible for me to withdraw myself from the world and its activities, as former Presidents are supposed to do.

As I shook hands and said good-bye to President Eisenhower on the Inauguration platform and walked toward the exit, I went over to former President Hoover and greeted him. Mr. Hoover said: "I think we ought to organize a former Presidents' club."

"Fine," I replied. "You be the president of the club and I will be the secretary."

We were at that moment the only two living former Presidents. And, without any formality, we have managed to keep in touch with each other since. Despite our basic political differences, we have respect for each other, and our relationship has always been in the best American tradition. Political contests sometimes lead to considerable heat and vigorous verbal exchanges, and I have been skinned many a time on things by political opponents. But I never carried over any grudges. President Hoover and I are the best of friends and I have great admiration for him. When campaigns are over and the people have made their decision, I believe personal feuds ought to end there. Our Republic certainly has grown mature enough for men in high places to rise above petulance and subordinate their capriciousness to their obligations as elected officials.

I was troubled about this on Inauguration Day. The world situation was ominous. Never before in our existence as a nation was it so necessary for an incoming President to be fully informed on all the issues and complicated responsibilities confronting him. I felt it was necessary for him to be in a position to assume full and effective charge of his office without the loss of a single day. For that reason I had directed, for the first time in the history of the nation, an orderly and carefully arranged turnover of government by all the departments to the incoming Administration. I was giving the incoming President fullest cooperation.

In that spirit, we had prepared, on Inauguration Day, to receive the President-elect and his family at an informal lunch at the White House. We were disappointed when the invitation was refused and the custom ignored. The President-elect chose to arrive at the White House when there was only enough time to go to the Capitol for the taking of the Presidential oath.

To avoid any further embarrassment, the lunch was cancelled. I then made myself ready to receive him. But he remained in his car at the portico of the White House. When I was informed that Mr. Eisenhower declined to come in, I went out to greet him and to escort him to the Capitol.

With but one exception, it had been the custom for the President-elect to call on the outgoing President before going to the Inauguration ceremonies. This of course did not include President-elect Roosevelt who, because of his physical condition, was unable to get out of his car and walk up the steps of the White House to call on outgoing President Hoover. The exception was Thomas Jefferson, and he could not very well have called on President Adams at the White House on Inaugural Day—because Adams had left in ill temper at midnight the day before just to avoid riding with Jefferson.

The journey in the parade down Pennsylvania Avenue was quite restrained—as far as the occupants of the Presidential car were concerned. We began our trip in silence. Then the President-elect volunteered to inform me: "I did not attend your Inauguration in 1948 out of consideration for you, because if I had been present I would have drawn attention away from you."

I was quick to reply: "You were not here in 1948 because I did not send for you. But if I *had* sent for you, you would have come."

The rest of the journey continued in silence.

I have been accused of quick temper. I prefer to think that I am quick to retort when provoked on a sensitive issue. But, having once expressed myself and made my position clear, I harbor no vengeful or bitter feelings toward anyone. I do not allow an unpleasant incident to distort my outlook. I would rather forget it and go on to other things.

I have but one purpose in telling of these Inaugural Day incidents. I had been provoked to lecture Candidate Eisenhower, during the 1952 campaign at Colorado Springs, for what I considered his failure to uphold the honor of General Marshall, who had been vilified as a traitor by Senators McCarthy and Jenner. This, no doubt, upset Eisenhower—as he should have been upset. But there is no disputing the facts in the matter. I felt strongly at the time that General Marshall should have been supported by General Eisenhower, who knew from association with him the character and greatness of Marshall. History, of course, will take care of that.

What was on my mind on that Inauguration Day, and since, has been regret that relentless grudges should so color the thinking and actions of men in trusted leadership. Only twice before had there been instances when the amenities in the change of Chief Executives had not been observed in agreeable spirit. As I mentioned before, John Adams, who succeeded George Washington, left the White House at midnight before Inaugural Day in order to avoid riding with Thomas Jefferson, when Jefferson took the oath as third President of the United States. Long after that, John Adams got to thinking about what he had done, and he was very sorry for it. And Chester Arthur, twenty-first President, rode in silence with Grover Cleveland, twenty-second President, at Cleveland's first Inauguration.

One of our difficulties in political campaigns in this country is that at times we make personal matters out of politics. I never had any bitter feelings about any of my opponents. In fact, each time I was elected to office, I was just as friendly with the opposition as I was with members of my own party.

There is no sense in carrying political animosity into personal affairs. In fact, in most of my campaigns, I found it best not to mention any of my opponents by name, which deprived them of any publicity I could give them. I did this primarily, however, because I was interested in stressing the issues and not persons or personalities.

AFTER shaking hands and saying good-bye to all my friends and associates on the Inaugural platform at the Capitol, I then began my journey back to private life. Mrs. Truman, Margaret and I went to the home of Dean Acheson for a short visit. I was pleasantly surprised to find a crowd of some three hundred people gathered in front of the Acheson home chanting, "We want Harry." Perhaps this group of partisans was not reconciled to the fact that the days of "We want Harry" were over. I went outside and waved goodbye. I felt that they were really there to pay their respects to the office of the President rather than to me personally.

I recall turning to John Snyder and saying, "What a great change can come to a man in a matter of moments. An hour ago anything I might have said would likely have been flashed around the world. Now I could talk for hours on any subject and no one would pay the slightest attention."

Snyder shook his head in disagreement.

On the way to the train from the Acheson home, we saw that the Inaugural parade was still going on. We hardly expected more than a handful of people at the station to see us off, but to my amazement a crowd of more than nine thousand people jammed the waiting room and the platforms between the tracks. I thought that this would be the last big crowd I would see greeting me anywhere. The people were friendly and warm, and I was deeply moved as they sang "Auld Lang Syne" and "For He's a Jolly Good Fellow."

It took a squad of police and Secret Service men to get Mrs. Truman and me on the train. I began to wonder about what lay ahead of me. This was the last time I would be shielded and protected by the Secret Service, who for eight years from the day I became Vice President and then President had been an integral part of my life twenty-four hours a day every day. I wondered whether my life henceforth would be one of peace and quiet, and I wondered how it would feel to be able to move about freely among my neighbors and among strangers without being under constant, if benevolent, surveillance.

It had been years since I had ridden in anything but an

all-Pullman train. I did have a private Presidential car assigned to me on this trip by the new President, and I appreciated the courtesy. Before turning in, I wanted a look at the coaches on the train. I went forward to the smoker. Some people did not recognize me at first, some seemed a little flustered. All were kind. In one of the cars the passengers started to stand up. But when I said, "Sit down or I'll go back," they settled down, laughing and slightly embarrassed. I was a little embarrassed myself. I was soon to find that people would insist on standing up wherever I appeared, and I began to realize that I would have to accept this special courtesy as a mark of respect for the office I once held. But from that evening on I did everything I could to discourage such things by explaining that I was now just plain Mr. Citizen.

I stayed in the smoker a short time and then returned to my car to get ready for bed. It had been quite a day. In the morning I woke up as the President of the United States. And now I was going to bed a private citizen. That night I slept soundly. But then I always sleep well.

I was completely unprepared for what was to happen when we arrived in Independence. I expected that there would probably be a reception of some kind, perhaps a hundred people or so. When we stepped off the train, the hundred had multiplied. There were people as far as you could see in every direction, shouting and waving. A band was playing the "Missouri Waltz," and everybody was yelling his head off.

I noticed a billboard beside the track. It read: "Independence—Home of President Truman." Someone had chalked in a big "Ex" before the word "President," and for some reason that seemed the only sensible, down-to-earth thing in sight.

Mrs. Truman looked as if she would not be able to talk. And so I spoke up for the family. I told them that I was happy to be home, and then I said to them: "I'm now home for good, and I mean it."

There were people all the way to 219 North Delaware Street, and there was a huge crowd waiting in front of our house. Later, I was told that there were upwards of ten thousand people at the Independence station and five thousand in front of the house. As we went inside the house, Mrs. Truman finally managed to say, "If this is what you get for all those years of hard work I guess it was worth it."

When I awoke the following morning, the room looked familiar but the light was wrong. Looking at the clock I saw that it was seven-thirty, which accounted for the light. I never sleep that late except when I am on vacation. This was not exactly a vacation. Yet—although at home and comfortable—I had a sense of being on a sort of temporary leave.

I took a bath, shaved and dressed and went downstairs. The morning paper was in the front yard. I picked it up and took it into the living room where I sat down to read. The front page news was mostly about our homecoming. Mayor Weatherford of Independence was quoted as telling the townsmen, "He will always be Mr. President to us."

I faced the problem of making the change from Mr. President to Mr. Citizen. Now it said in print that I was always going to be Mr. President. People wanted to address me as Mr. President, I realized, both in recognition of the office I had held and because of their own sense of participation with it.

The second morning I was up at five-thirty—an hour which had been fixed by my life at the farm and not in Washington, although I had continued the habit there. It was only now that it seemed strange not to find a Secret Service man in the corridor near the door of my bedroom. I felt that a certain measure of personal freedom and privacy had been restored to me, and I liked it.

I dressed and started on my usual morning walk before breakfast. Again, the sense of being left to myself, without being watched and followed by men whose duty it was to protect me when I was President, was even more striking. More than any other single thing, this marked the abrupt change in my life. At that early hour, it was a pleasure to exchange greetings with my neighbors and to be able to do so in an informal way.

During this walk, I let my mind run free with thoughts of things mainly personal. I could now think a little more about what was ahead of me—without the involvement of the world and the duties and pressures of official life. I began recalling what had happened to other Presidents who survived their terms of office and returned to private life. It was natural and necessary for me to do so because I had to face up to the fact that I had to make a living.

Those of our Presidents who were rich men before going to the White House went home to their estates. Those of modest means had to do the best they could to earn a living. Either way, the country had never made plans to draw on the invaluable experience of former Presidents for further public service. Certainly the nation did not and should not wish its former Presidents to use their special experience for private and personal gain. I had to find a way of working again as a citizen without permitting myself to be used by any private interests because of the great office I once held.

On returning home from my walk, I found the morning newspaper lying at the front door. This time, the newspaper brought me back sharply to the world I had just left behind me, but I had known all along that I could never and would never detach myself from active interest and participation in the affairs of the world and the nation.

Whatever I was going to do to make a living, there was one decision that I had made during the last months of my stay in the White House. The rest of my life was to be spent, in large measure, teaching our young people the meaning of democracy as exemplified in the Republic of the United States. I was going to devote time to writing and to establishing a library where the papers I had gathered as President could be made available to students and to the public.

I would make myself available to schools and colleges to lecture on American government and American history. And I would give preference to the smaller colleges and schools less centrally located, which did not have vast libraries and research facilities. I thought it would be best to talk to students in the Middle West and Far West. I hoped I would be able to establish a library in the Middle West for research on the Presidency.

As the days went by, friends wondered whether I would be able to regain the composure and serenity that I looked for in private life. Having been conditioned by the Presidency to deal with events and problems as they occurred, could I avoid being disturbed, they asked, by what was going on in the world now that I could no longer do anything about it? Of course, I could not help but be disturbed, and that was natural.

I always took the view that the Presidency is a gift of the people who elect the President for a limited time. When that period is over, he has not changed as a person from what he was before, and I thought it should be easy to go back to private life. Having returned, the former President ought to continue to do whatever he can to contribute to the welfare of the country. And the welfare of the country rests on the basis that the government of the United States is a government installed for the purpose of giving the people a chance to do what they think is right.

The people have often made mistakes, but given time and the facts, they will make the corrections.

At any rate, I have always believed that a fellow who started on a farm and went through the whole political set-up from precinct to Presidency ought to quit when it was time to quit. Then he should go back and see if he could not give the people more information on what makes the greatest government in the history of the world run. They say I'm a fanatic on the subject and I guess I am.

2

Back Home
in Independence

M OST people never stop to think about what happens
to a man who has been President of the United
States. The day he is elected President he suddenly finds
himself at the top of the world, where he sits for a while,
holding the destinies of millions in his hands, making decisions that change the course of history, conferring with
rulers and the leaders of nations. Then just as suddenly he is
again at the level of John Jones, who lives next door.

The procedure is so firmly fixed in our tradition that we
do not give it a second thought. We believe that anybody
can be President of the United States and that when he is
through, he can go back to being just anybody again. I cannot say I feel exactly that way about it. It has not been that
simple for me. Back home in Independence, I discovered
that it was not easy to assume the role of Mr. Citizen.

I had to go through the process of again becoming a
member of the community where I was raised. After nearly

eight years in the White House and ten years in the Senate, I found myself right back where I started in Independence, Missouri.

My return to ordinary citizenship began a new life filled with new meaning. After all the crowds and furor, the whole business did not seem so easy. Were the people going to let me become a private citizen? Or was I still going to have to live up to the title of Mr. President that the people insisted on using?

I spent nearly fifteen years living and working on a farm. It was a wonderful experience. It taught me agriculture, how things grow and how to take care of them. I learned those things the hard way, by experience and by the study of reports of the Department of Agriculture of the United States and of the Colleges of Agriculture in Missouri and Iowa.

Those years on the farm also taught me some diplomacy. I had numerous aunts and uncles and some thirty cousins. These kinfolk were all on good terms with me—but hardly ever with one another. It was my duty to be the family peacemaker. I was also frequently called upon to fix up differences between the neighbors. We exchanged work with them, and they with us and with one another. Naturally, there was some occasional disagreement. It was my role to help them get along.

I also got the habit on the farm of getting up early in the morning. In those days farmers had to make use of every daylight hour. I have never been able to break that early rising habit. When I was in the army, I was the fellow whose duty it was to wake up the bugler. Then I would go off and think about the rest of my day's work as a first lieutenant. Morning is the best time for solid thinking.

Now back home, I have been running on the same schedule I have followed for years: up at five-thirty, dress, then downstairs to read the paper the boy flips over the fence. This is the first paper of the day; later, there are four or five other paper from different parts of the country. You cannot get all the facts from just one newspaper, and unless you have the facts, you cannot make proper judgments about what is going on. You should never form judgments from front page headlines. As with a contract, the fine print on the inside pages should be carefully studied.

In the spring and summer, I take the newspaper around to the back porch and settle down with it, along with the correspondence I have not had a chance to look at the day before. I sit there for an hour, alone, feeling the sun slanting in at me, and putting my thoughts straight.

In the winter I do the same thing in the living room. Then I go for a walk. I began taking these walks when I first went to Washington as a senator in 1935. And since these walks seemed to keep me fit then, in spite of all the sitting around I had to do, I have kept them up.

Except for the absence of the Secret Service men, my walks are about the same as they were when I was in the White House. I usually go out the front way, and now I have to stop in the vestibule to press the button that opens the latch of the front gate. That iron fence, with the locked gates around the house, was put up in 1947, two years after I became President. President Hoover advised me to have it done. "If you don't," he said, "they'll tear the place down." ("They" being souvenir hunters.) Hoover had some bad experiences with "them" and said they once walked off with some of his doorknobs.

That fence always reminds me of what some smart alecs of those days after World War I used to say: "The French fought for liberty, the British fought to control the seas, but the Americans fought for souvenirs."

IN the weeks and months that followed my return from Washington, there were usually several cars occupied by sightseers outside the front gate, waiting for me at seven o'clock in the morning. That was the time I left for the office which I had set up in Kansas City, eight miles from Independence. One day there was a car parked in front of the house with baggage piled all over it.

"Is this where Truman lives?" the man at the wheel shouted at me.

I said it was, and he called: "Are you Truman?"

I answered I was.

"Well," he said, "me and the old lady are on a motor trip all the way from the island of Maui in Hawaii. Been all over the country, but seeing you walk out of that house, big as life, tops everything else we have seen. Would you mind if I just got a picture of you standing there?"

If anyone in Washington had told me that this sort of thing was just as common after you left the White House as it was before, I might have suspected that he was trying to tempt me to run for another term. Once when a photographer was assigned to take pictures of our house, he came over about five thirty in the morning. He was prowling

Inaugural Day, January 20, 1953. I come out to receive President-elect Eisenhower on the portico of the White House. Below, the President-elect and I return greetings just as we leave for the procession up Pennsylvania Avenue to the Capitol.

There was nothing to say except goodbye, but it was heartwarming to see such a big crowd assembled at the station to see us off when we left Washington after the Inaugural ceremonies to return to private life. In the picture at lower left, I am back home in Independence on January 21. Our neighbors made it a most happy occasion for Mrs. Truman and myself. The cartoon below speaks for itself—but I couldn't help adding a comment.

"O.K., so you grow up to be President, and you even get re-elected, that's still only eight years. What do you do with the rest of your life?"

The Saturday Review

God only knows!!!

HST

My first early morning walk in Independence on my return to private life in 1953 (upper left). Usually, reporters come along looking for news, and most of the time they get it if their legs hold out. Not all who start are there at the finish of these 120-paces-a-minute press conferences, though. When I am visiting in New York, taxi drivers stop me on my early morning walk and think I should be riding instead of walking. Many drivers with friendly smiles yell as they drive by, "When are you going to ride again, Harry?" But I tell them I walk for my health before breakfast.

Wide World Photos

United Press International Photo

Above, some of the messages sent to me when I was in the Research Hospital in Kansas City for surgery. I tried to say thanks for the tens of thousands of letters wishing me well. Below, I pitch the opening ball for the Athletics in Kansas City on April 15, 1955. I used to pitch for the Senators in Washington.

United Press International Photo

My favorite animal is the mule. He has more horse sense than a horse. He knows when to stop eating—and he knows when to stop working.

In Paris, I take my usual morning walk—to the surprise of some Americans at a famous sidewalk café near the Place de l'Opera. This was on the occasion of our European trip in the spring of 1956.

This is a picture which His Holiness, Pope Pius XII, asked to be taken during our visit to the Vatican on May 20, 1956. I considered Pope Pius XII the greatest statesman in the Papacy in two hundred years.

In Venice, we do what every tourist does. Later, we headed for the Doges' Palace for a refresher on history. This is one city where they thought I would give up my early morning walk. But I fooled them and found some terra firma for my walk.

United Press International Photo

Above, during our stay in London we visit the Tower of London and talk to a Beefeater. A highlight of our European trip was our get-together with Sir Winston and Lady Churchill at their home in Chartwell, Kent. The great man and I took the occasion to talk alone about the past and the future, not liking the current trend of things. From the left, in the picture below, are: Mary and Sarah, daughters of Sir Winston; Mrs. Truman; Sir Winston; HST; Lady Churchill; Lord Beaverbrook and Rt. Hon. Christopher Soames.

United Press International Photo

Mrs. Truman and I attend the 1956 Democratic Convention in Chicago. They have just made the decision to nominate Adlai E. Stevenson for President.

I break ground with a gold shovel for the Truman Library in Independence on May 8, 1955. The building was completed in 1957, and the dedication ceremonies were held on July 6 of that year. Below is a photograph of the Library as it appears today.

The office of the President, as it appeared during my Administration, is reproduced in one room of the Truman Library. If you visit the Library and press a button just outside the door of this room, you will hear a record of my voice telling about this room and how it was used.

United Press International Photo

Just before the dedication of the Library, I greet Mrs. Eleanor Roosevelt, Speaker of the House Sam Rayburn, Senator Lyndon Johnson of Texas, Chief Justice Earl Warren, Basil O'Connor and Governor G. Mennen Williams of Michigan who came to Independence for the dedication ceremonies. Taking a trip through the Library with me below on that day are Former President Hoover, Chief Justice Warren, Mr. O'Connor and Congressman Halleck of Indiana.

Harry S. Truman Library Photograph

Harry S. Truman Library Photograph

Adlai E. Stevenson, Judge F. Ryan Duffy and Jake Moore visit the Truman Library and view the case containing the two Bibles on which I took my oath of office as President on April 12, 1945, and on January 20, 1949. Mr. Stevenson noted that the Bible was opened at the Book of Exodus and commented, "Why Exodus? I thought you were going in and not going out?"

United Press International Photo

A sort of coming-out party on December 7, 1959 for Democratic Presidential prospects at a banquet in New York in celebration of Mrs. Eleanor Roosevelt's seventy-fifth birthday. Most of the prospects are here in this picture, although several entries had yet to show. From the left are: Governor Robert F. Meyner of New Jersey, Senator Hubert Humphrey, Governor Leroy Collins of Florida, Governor G. Mennen Williams of Michigan, myself, Senator Stuart Symington of Missouri, Senator John F. Kennedy of Massachusetts and California Governor Edmund G. Brown.

I announce the forthcoming publication of this book at a press conference in the Library at Independence in the summer of 1959. The picture in the background is San Juan Hill at Santiago, Cuba, where Theodore Roosevelt did not ride. Everyone walked up this hill.

around the lawn, looking for a good spot from which to take a picture, when a tourist car pulled up in front, and a man hopped out.

"Hey," I heard him say to the photographer, "you work around this place?"

I had let the photographer in on the lawn while I went in to read the newspaper.

"Well," said the photographer, "I do in a way."

"Good," said the tourist, "I want to get a couple of snaps of where Truman lives. The joint looks kind of dead, but with you in the picture that will give it some kind of life. Mind getting over there and acting as if you were pulling flowers or something?"

The photographer obliged, although I could see that he looked a little embarrassed.

Sometimes whole delegations stand outside looking over the fence—school children, Girl Scouts, all kinds of people from all parts of the country and even from foreign lands. I realize that they come to see "that man from Missouri." And I try, when I am at home, not to disappoint them. I wave to them, and when I have time I exchange greetings with them and occasionally pose for a picture.

Many funny incidents have occurred with tourists. For example, one woman asked me to pose with her for a photograph. I said jokingly, "Madam, what is your husband going to say when he sees us together in a picture?"

"Oh," she said, "don't worry about him, he's the one who is taking the picture."

"Well," I said, "I'm glad he is here. Tell you what—I'll pose with him and you take the picture." She did, though she looked kind of surprised for a minute.

In all the years since I left the White House, I have wondered why so many people come from so far away and take so much trouble to look at the house where I live. Perhaps it is because once a man has been President he becomes an object of curiosity like those other notorious Missouri characters, Mark Twain and Jesse James.

Shortly after I returned, the governor of the state insisted on assigning a highway patrol sergeant to look after me when I began to move about Independence and Kansas City. All the public officials were kind, but they found out, as I knew they would, that I did not need police protection. Everyone is friendly.

THERE are too many people who seem to feel that one of the uses to which they can put their former President is for him to help them make their personal decisions. They figure that as long as I had to make so many decisions while I was President, it must be easier for me than for them.

Some people do not seem to understand that it is one thing to make decisions as President and an entirely different business to make decisions as a private citizen, especially for someone else. In the White House, I never allowed myself to think that Harry Truman from Independence, Missouri, was a person deciding the fate of the world. I was deciding as President, and not as an individual thinking in terms of what he would prefer as an individual.

I always made the distinction between the office of President and the person of the President. That may seem to some a fine distinction, but I am glad I made it. Otherwise

I might be suffering today from the same kind of "importance" complex that some people have come down with. Washington is full of big shots whose already inflated egos go up with a touch of "Potomac fever." I tried very hard to escape that ludicrous disease.

When it comes to deciding things, I might as well confess that since arriving home I have had trouble arriving at one or two decisions of my own. Lunch, for example. I do not like to eat alone. But setting up a routine at the beginning was a little awkward. I was an ordinary citizen again, but I was also an ordinary citizen who had been President, and sometimes that plain fact could be embarrassing to me and to other people. It still is.

During the first few months I managed to solve the problem in part by lunching every noon with the same small group in one of the private dining rooms in the Hotel Muehlebach—the room we still call the "Hideaway." I continue to meet with friends from out of town in the Hideaway for lunch.

But in those early months, I figured I would have to branch out. One day I telephoned a friend and told him I would like to take him to lunch at the Pickwick Hotel, around the corner from my first office in the Federal Reserve Bank Building.

This is how he reported his experience to one of my friends in New York: "I'd never been to the Pickwick in my life for lunch. But the 'Boss' wanted it so I said okay. We went into the lunchroom to the right of the main entrance— it's got a food counter and a dozen or so tables. Everybody in the place did a double-take, and the waitress who showed us where to sit nearly fell over herself. Then the autograph hunters and the folks with hands stretched out for shaking began to close in. All in all it was quite a lunch. Only it was really more like old home week!

"The next day the 'Boss' called me up again, saying, 'I'm taking you to lunch again today. I'll be around at twelve.' And at twelve sharp, he arrived in that police car he was being driven around in at the time, and off we go to some chili joint I never heard of. This kept up all week. We would pile into the car, dash off to a restaurant, eat in a hurry and back he would go to work. Usually I had had lunch at my own office or at the Hotel Muehlebach or at the Kansas City Club.

"The 'Boss' is a member of the Kansas City Club, too—one of four who have been made honorary members. President Eisenhower, General of the Armies Bradley, and the late Judge John Caskie Collet were the other three.

"I wondered why he never mentioned going there to lunch until it occurred to me that about ninety-five per cent of the membership is Republican—and when I say Republican I mean Republican.

"Anyway, I finally suggested it. He hesitated, and then said, 'All right, if you want to.'

"I'll never forget that day at the Kansas City Club. Men who used to damn him up and down when he was in the White House flocked around to shake his hand. They were all glad to see him, and he had more fun than a barrel of monkeys. For the first time in two solid weeks he didn't rush back to his office right after eating.

"Next morning, I got a call from him, saying, 'How about lunch at the Kansas City Club today?'

" 'Fine,' I said, congratulating myself, and for the next

four days we went there every noon. By this time his tendency to shy away was gone, but there was still one last hurdle—to go to the Club by himself. This he overcame, but not without first getting an assist from another friend."

THE fact is, I do like to have lunch at the Kansas City Club. There is no conversation so sweet as that of former political enemies. The way I look at it, I have been blessed in both my enemies and my friends. And, of course, there are not many pleasures to compare with sitting down to lunch at the Club or at the Muehlebach or anywhere with close friends.

While I had my office in Kansas City, I would go back there after lunch and catch up on phone calls or letters that had come in the second mail. At about three o'clock, I would leave the office to be driven back to Independence. Once or twice a week I would find Bess playing bridge with friends or relatives. The other days she was there alone. In either case I would go upstairs and take a nap, as Dr. Wallace Graham ordered. He promised me another twenty years if I followed the rules, and I did not want to disappoint him. I was then sixty-eight years old.

The house seemed quiet and too big, with just Bess and Vietta Garr, our cook, who did not live in the house. We missed Margaret, but she had her own career and had to live in New York. I did not complain. But we kept in close touch by telephone. There is an extension line upstairs, and every day after my nap I picked up my phone, Bess picked up the other and we called Margaret—or, if we missed connections, she called us.

We got in the habit of doing this in Washington while Margaret was traveling around making personal concert appearances. In those days we used to have regular telephone parties, bringing in all the uncles and the cousins and the aunts, with everybody putting in his two cents' or two dollars' worth. Our family always has been closely knit, even if strained at the seams in places, and Alexander Bell's invention helped us maintain the illusion of being together physically.

After getting back in our routine in Independence, Bess and I almost invariably ate early dinner, usually alone or with friends or relatives who lived nearby. It was good to have neighbors join us again, either for dinner or later in the evening, to hash over local gossip. We had several television sets but we did not use them much, or the radio either, except for special programs and, of course, to watch Margaret any time she was on a television show.

During the last few years in Washington we cut down drastically on outside functions. This gave us more time to read, although personally I could never find time enough to read all the things I wanted to. In Independence, most of our evenings are spent reading. Bess favors detective stories. I prefer history and biographies, although I have developed an interest in whodunits as well.

When we were asked out to dinner, we would try to go, if we knew the people. But with one or two exceptions we avoided "functions." The exceptions convinced us that we had better avoid them. One was a basketball game to which a friend asked us. It was a windup game of a big intercollegiate tournament they hold in Kansas City each year. Bess likes basketball, and so do I, and we decided to go.

As soon as we were seated, they turned the spotlight on us, and about three hundred people stormed our box, pencils and autograph blanks in hand. It finally took many ushers to ward them off. They had to announce over the loud-speaker that no autographs would be handed out while the game was in progress. Even so, the more rugged members of the crowd managed to get through to our box with their requests. We never saw the finish of the game. Our host lost his nerve and smuggled us out with five minutes left to go. He said he was afraid that if we did not leave then we might never be able to get out. After that, we decided we had better stay home for a while and go to bed early.

It seemed strange to some people that, after leaving the White House, I should need an office, with its heavy burden of personal expense. There were reasons why an office was necessary. For one thing, I received many letters which I felt deserved an answer, even when they were from people I did not know. I have always believed that if a person goes to the trouble of writing a letter, even a critical letter, I should answer or at least acknowledge it.

Then there were visitors to see, people who wanted to express their good wishes. Many came out of a natural curiosity to see what I looked like in real life and to hold a conversation with me. I wanted to see as many of them as I could.

I also wanted a place to do some writing and to house a staff to assist me in my research. I wanted to record the facts I knew at first hand about the important events of my Administration. There was a big difference between the facts as I saw them and as they had been presented by the press and radio. Much of the disparity arose not because reporters deliberately tried to misinform the public but because they were in no position to know all that went on.

Soon after leaving the White House I started negotiations for the publication of my Memoirs. I also found myself immersed in a flood of invitations and needed help. I was asked to attend everything from national conventions to church suppers. And the range of visitors was astonishing. A man who had paid five hundred dollars for a bust of me by a Polish sculptor wanted to sell it to me for "a price to be agreed upon." A college graduate wanted to know the best way to get into politics. The founder of a new cult thought I ought to join. A boy wanted my autograph to help recruit seventy-five new Cub Scouts. I had carelessly mentioned to a columnist that I was looking for a silver dollar minted in 1924—Margaret's birth year—and silver dollars were brought in and mailed in by the dozen.

It really surprised me that only about half of one per cent of the letters were from cranks. I made it my business to come in early and be the first to see the mail. I wanted to be sure to see all the mail—even crackpot and vilifying letters. I had learned during my years in the White House that my well-meaning staff sorted out and withheld offensive letters in order to spare my feelings.

But I told them then—and stressed it again in my Kansas City office—that they were not doing me a service by keeping from me the violently critical letters. I could learn as much from those letters what was in some people's minds as I could from any other source. Now that I was no longer President, I expected the offensive communications to continue, if not to increase, and I did not want to be pampered and over-protected by my staff.

What surprised me was that there was so little serious criticism in the mail. Some of the writers had disagreed with my policies as President and were frank in saying so, but as a rule they wished me well. A New Hampshire Republican even sent me a ten dollar contribution to the fund I was trying to raise for a building to house my Presidential papers and provide a place where the history of the Presidency could be studied. It was an experience for me to see how many Republicans did write to me in a pleasant vein and offer contributions for the building fund.

The thing that was most unbelievable was the number of different jobs that were proposed to me. The offers began to arrive before I left the White House; like the letters, they were many and varied. A chain of clothing stores wanted me to be its vice president at an annual salary in six figures. A sewing machine company wanted me to be chairman of the board, also at a salary in six figures, but with no work to do except to appear in public ceremonies for the company. The chief executive of a motion picture company called on me to try to interest me in a merger of several producing companies, saying that the deal could be consummated only if I agreed to join and head it up. He offered a fabulous salary and added that I could name my own terms. Several oil companies thought I would be a good man to have around. One proposal of an eight-year contract, requiring only an hour's "work," guaranteed over a half million dollars.

I turned down all of those offers. I knew that they were not interested in hiring Harry Truman, the person, but what they wanted to hire was the former President of the United States. I could never lend myself to any transaction, however respectable, that would commercialize on the prestige and the dignity of the office of the Presidency.

Some of the visitors to my office in Kansas City reminded me of the old days when I was in local politics. Some asked for advice, some for minor favors and some wanted me to use my influence to get them jobs or to keep them in jobs. Whenever I could, of course, I always helped. But I often jokingly said, "I'm sorry, but I'm out of a job myself."

I began to notice that people took it for granted that being President automatically deprives you of the ability to do anything for yourself. Even some of my closest friends suffer from this delusion. An intimate friend who should have known better was amazed the first time he saw me pick up a phone and dial a number for myself. Others seemed to be equally astonished when I carried a sackful of mail out of the Independence post office, put a coin in the parking meter, hailed a cab, or got my hair cut in a barbershop. What a way to feel about a man whose mother used to boast that he could lay out the straightest corn row in Jackson County!

As a matter of fact, I would have done more things for myself in the White House if the people around there had let me. The trouble was they were always grabbing bags and opening doors before I could get at them.

WHEN it got out that Mrs. Truman and I were going to drive to Washington by ourselves the first summer we were back home, the news nearly bowled our friends over. They organized a regular filibuster, telephoned me at home and the office, stopped me on the street and got at me over the lunch table, trying to talk me out of the trip. I am kind of stubborn, though, and since no one could give me what I thought was a sensible reason why we should not go, we went.

The last time Bess and I had traveled together by car was after the Democratic convention in 1944. Nobody worried much then, when I had just been nominated as Vice President, and we made it all right.

Well, we made the trip, just the two of us. But we've never tried it again! We ran into some surprising experiences on the road to Washington.

3

Washington Revisited

I LIKE to take trips—any kind of trip. They are about the only recreation I have besides reading. And traveling has taught me almost as much as I have learned from books. I have often thought that perhaps if I had not gone to France as an artillery officer during World War I, I might not have gotten into politics at all.

I entered politics partly as a result of my war services, at the urging and with the help of my war companions. My experiences in France led to an interest in roads and to the belief that public highways could be beautiful as well as useful, and this conviction came to play an important role in my early political services. When Jackson County voted ten million dollars for the construction of 336 miles of roads, it became my responsibility as the presiding officer of the county to see that they were built. And so, as a result of my travels in France and my observations of roads at home, I had a good idea of how these roads should be built. They should be durable, and made attractive with roadside landscaping and with trees lining both sides.

Later, when the county commissioned me to build a new courthouse, I did not just sit in a chair and study architectural plans. I traveled all over the country by car, looking at courthouses and drawing my own conclusions. The result was one of the most efficient structures of its kind built by any county.

Years later, as chairman of the Senate committee looking all over the country into the vast industrial production for war, I did considerable traveling with other members of the committee to investigate the National Defense Program. As candidate for Vice President, on the ticket with Franklin D. Roosevelt in 1944, I assumed the major burden of travel for both of us.

In 1947, I made a cross-country tour, with stopovers in villages and towns as well as cities. I was reporting to the people on what I was trying to do as President, and my opponents dubbed it a "whistle-stop" campaign. No other President had traveled so far to talk to the people, especially in a non-election year. I think I learned as much from the people as they may have learned from me, and this trip not only resulted in a pattern for future action but sharpened my views on many current problems.

And then, of course, I did a little traveling in 1948—in a campaign I supposedly had no hope of winning. And that resulted in a lot of arm-chair politicians going out of business.

You learn what people are saying and thinking when you get around among them. You sometimes get surprises, as I got on our first trip after leaving the White House. Mrs. Truman, Margaret and I stopped over in San Francisco on our way to Hawaii in March, 1953, to be the guests of the Edwin W. Pauleys on their Coconut Island. This provided an experience I would not have missed for anything.

We were supposed to have dinner at the home of George Killion, head of the steamship company whose liner we were to travel on. The chauffeur who was driving us got into the right neighborhood—but picked the wrong house. I rang the bell, and an unmistakably Republican-looking gentleman opened the door.

"Does Mr. Killion live here?" I asked.

"No," he said and drew back to study me. "By the way," he added, "I hope your feelings won't be hurt—but you look exactly like Harry Truman."

"I hope yours won't either," I replied, "but I *am* Harry Truman."

As I say, travel can be broadening. I still treasure the memory of the expression on that gentleman's face. Incidentally, he lived only a block away from Killion's house, but couldn't tell us where Killion lived! That could never have happened in Independence.

BUT to get back to the experiences of our trip east. In the summer of 1953, Bess and I decided to go to Washington to see some of our old dispossessed friends there, then on to Philadelphia for a speech I had to make to the Reserve Officers, and finally to New York to see Margaret.

We were determined to drive despite the efforts of our

friends to talk us out of it. After our return from Hawaii we became the owners of two new cars, one for Bess and one for me. I was looking forward to giving mine a real tryout.

Incidentally, I had not had mine more than a couple of weeks when, driving through the narrow back gate of our home in Independence, I scraped all the chromium off one side of it. That gate always reminds me of the camel and the needle's eye, and I thought I would never hear the last of it from Bess. But then one morning she called me at the office, and her voice sounded a little unhappy.

"Anything the matter?" I asked.

"Well," she said, "I hate to tell you this, but the truth is I was coming through the gate this morning and scraped the chromium off the side of my car."

After that neither of us mentioned chromium again.

BEFORE starting for Washington, I took out the road map and figured the distance—exactly 1050 miles from my garage door to the door of the Senate garage. I decided on the best places to stop over on the way, as I always used to do. Up to this time, I had not had much luck at living like the plain ordinary citizen I had hoped to become on leaving the White House. I thought that this holiday would give me a chance to do so at last. The press knew I intended to make the trip, but they did not know exactly when or how. Only our closest friends knew that, and they were pledged not to tell.

So on the road, at least, we expected to enjoy the pleasures of traveling incognito. We might have succeeded, too —at least across the state of Missouri—except for a small incident involving our speedometer. We had talked about who was going to do the driving—Bess thinks I drive too fast and I think she goes too slow—and finally we hit on a compromise. I was to do the driving, but not as fast as usual. Anyway, we started off at seven-thirty one hot Friday morning, and we had not gone very far before Bess leaned forward and said, "What does the speedometer say?"

"Fifty-five," I said.

"Do you think I'm losing my eyesight? Slow down!"

So we slowed down.

Naturally, at fifty-five miles an hour, everything on the road—it was a state road in open country, laid out especially so that you could make time—began passing us. Not only that, but since we were going so slowly, they had a chance to look us over. Pretty soon the shouted greetings started: "Hi, Harry!"—"Hey! Wasn't that Harry Truman?"—"Where you going, Harry?"

"Well," I said, "there goes our incognito—and I don't mean a part of the car."

We stopped for lunch in a restaurant in Mark Twain's home town—Hannibal by *the* River, the old Mississippi. The girl who waited on us did not seem to know who we were— at least she did not drop her order book or anything—and I was just beginning to feel like a private citizen again, when in came three county judges. One of them looked at me, looked away, looked back, and walked over to our table.

"Aren't you President Truman?" he asked.

"That is what they used to call me," I said. At this point, the waitress *did* get flustered.

From then on it was the same thing over and over again. When we reached Decatur, Illinois, where we had planned to spend the night, a man in a filling station recognized us and called the local newspaper. After the reporters came running, the chief of police assigned two policemen and two detectives to see us to our motel.

The following day, we lunched with friends at Indianapolis and then drove to Wheeling, West Virginia, where we put up at the same hotel where Bess and I stopped twenty years ago. We arrived rather late, and just as we were settling down, the phone rang. It was the manager wanting to know why I had not notified him in advance of our coming.

"Call me tomorrow morning," I said, "and I will tell you."

Next morning the lobby was crowded with photographers and reporters all set to greet us. The manager bustled up, and I said: "You asked me why I did not let you know we were coming. Take a look around. *This* is why."

Everyone was most pleasant and cordial to us. The waitresses and bellboys wanted autographs and the manager could not have been more courteous. However, it was not until we pulled into Frederick, Maryland, in the afternoon, that the press really showed up in force. Margaret, who had come down to Washington to stay with us at the Mayflower, had told the press, with my permission, to meet us at Frederick if they insisted on seeing us.

The press caught up with us at the filling station in Frederick where I had always filled up in times past. I was reminded of the time my mother visited us at the White House. I had wanted her to meet some of these same press correspondents, but I was a little uncertain how she would take to the idea, so I put off saying anything about it until I was leading her from the plane into the midst of them.

Then I said: "Mama, these are photographers and reporters. They want to take your picture and talk to you."

"Fiddlesticks," she said. "They don't want to see *me*. If I had known this would happen, I would have stayed home!"

There on the road in Frederick, I felt the same way she did.

As soon as we arrived in Washington, the calendar seemed to have been turned back a year. My old staff was there to meet me, as were most of the members of my Cabinet, and many judges, senators and congressmen were all on hand to pick up again where they had left off in January.

It seemed like a dream to relive such an experience. For one solid week, the illusion of those other days in Washington was maintained perfectly. The suite we stayed in at the Mayflower could have been the White House; many of the visitors were the same. Everything seemed just as it used to be—the taxi drivers shouting hello along the line of my morning walks, the dinners at night with the men and women I had worked with for years, the conferences, the tension, excitement, the feeling of things happening and going to happen—all the same. I was deeply moved by the spontaneous expression of good will shown me.

It would have gone to my head more than it did, I guess, if I had not remembered one thing that my mother once said. During her last illness at Grandview, our old Battery "D" Chaplain, Father Tiernan, went to see her and, hoping to cheer her up, said: "Mrs. Truman, you must be very proud that a son of yours is in the White House."

After thinking it over for a minute, she said: "Well, yes, but I have got another son who lives down the road a piece —and I'm just as proud of him."

4

Concerning
Adlai Stevenson

I NEVER had any sentimental attachment for the Potomac
River, either when I lived in Washington or when I went
back to it for a visit. But the river served me well when I
used the U.S.S. "Williamsburg" as the floating White House.
I sailed for the last time on this Presidential yacht on a trip
down the Potomac for a weekend of reflection soon after the
elections of 1952.

Having given instructions to all the departments of the
government to begin the process of making the turn-over to
the President-designate, I wanted to do some thinking about
the future of the Democratic party and what I was going to
do after January 20, 1953. I took with me a small group of
trusted personal advisers and friends.

On occasion, the "Williamsburg" had served as the floating White House, allowing me to get away from the routine
of the Executive Office, and enabling me to combine a certain amount of relaxation with work. Often, on these short

trips, officials of the Administration and leaders of Congress accompanied me for consultations. A President needs to get away from time to time from the confining environment of the White House to gain perspective.

This last trip was in no way a political post-mortem. As the campaign of 1952 had developed, I had not been unprepared for the outcome. What concerned me now was what kind of leadership the Democratic party would get from Adlai Stevenson, who, although defeated, was now the titular head of the party.

I was ready to take my position in the ranks and to do all I could to help him in this future role, although Stevenson had made it clear, during the campaign, that he preferred to detach himself from the man in the White House and the party headquarters in Washington. Stevenson, of course, had the right to do what he did, but in my opinion he only helped the opposition and hurt himself.

The way the campaign was conducted cost the party at least three to four million votes. The loss of these votes to the Republicans provided them with such a sweeping victory statistically that they misjudged the true temper of the country. As a result, the victorious Republicans undertook to make drastic revisions in domestic and foreign policy which led to grave errors they have been trying to repair ever since.

In assessing the results of 1952, we have to take into account that General Eisenhower was a glamorous military hero, glorified by the press. And he was campaigning at a time when many people were perhaps tired of the strains of wartime and the sacrifices they had been making for so many years. They were susceptible to inducements to escape from the tensions and anxieties of responsibilities that were still a long way from being fulfilled. The dangerous and misleading hopes that were aroused by Eisenhower's siren call over Korea—where after seven long years we still have no peace but only a precarious truce with our forces pinned down and exposed to danger—was an effective appeal for votes. Only a military man could have successfully exploited such a situation for partisan political advantage.

The circumstances that had led me not to be a candidate in 1952 were many, but certainly I was not stepping out for reasons of physical fitness. My doctors assured me that I was in excellent physical condition and could go on if I wanted to. They were right. The fact is that I have continued to maintain a vigorous schedule of work and travel since I came home.

It is obvious that I was not going to retire to pasture and fade completely from the political scene. But whatever I had in mind for myself, and whatever I may have preferred to do, I thought it was time for the party to develop new leadership.

The first thing I did on that last trip on the "Williamsburg" was to outline to my associates my thinking on the succession to the leadership of the party. I decided to send a message to Stevenson pledging my full support of his leadership. I wanted to leave no doubt in his mind that, as a former President, I was available to him at all times in an advisory capacity.

I felt that when the Democratic party in convention nominated a man to be its candidate for President, that candidate became the new leader and he remained the leader until the next convention. Of course, I was disappointed that during the campaign the nominee of the party had not understood the necessity of giving unqualified support to the policies of the incumbent Democratic President. Unless there was something basically wrong, the candidate should have gone along with the policies of the Administration.

The question arises as to what happens if the candidate fails to do so. Well, there is not very much that the President can do about it. The President could only regret it but he could not even mention it during the campaign.

Notwithstanding all this, I intended to recognize and support Stevenson as the party leader and therefore lost no time in sending the message to him through a trusted friend. But as time went on, it was a difficult matter to get Stevenson to realize fully that, as the nominee of the Democratic party, he was its leader.

I HAVE been asked whether Stevenson's reluctance to take over active direction could have been due to the circumstance that there was a living former President, whose opinions and advice were still being sought by many members of the party. I certainly tried to make him and everyone else in the party understand that the leadership was his. There should have been no hesitation on his part, because there was nothing to prevent consultation between him and the former President.

But Stevenson continued to remain aloof. His failure to pick up the reins of leadership brought about a period of confusion and drift and factionalism within our party. To fill the vacuum there were two developments. The first was constructive. An advisory committee was set up which could function as the public voice of the party and on which many of the top party leaders served, including Mr. Stevenson and myself. The second development led to difficulties. The national chairman of the party and the national committee expanded their roles to include policy-making, thus usurping authority that was not properly theirs but belonged to the party convention or the party nominee. It is the party convention that lays down policy, and the only functions of a national chairman are to carry out that policy and to make the necessary arrangements for the next convention.

THE situation did not improve as time went on. In July, 1955, Mr. Stevenson came to see me, at his request, at the Blackstone Hotel in Chicago to talk about the affairs of the party. I came directly to the point and said: "Why don't you announce yourself now as a Presidential candidate, so that we can get a head start? Now is the time to do the necessary advance work that we were prevented from doing in 1952 when you held off until the last moment."

Then I added: "If you decide to run, I will back you and do all I can to help you. I have no one else in mind. But you have got to make up your mind *now*. Delay will only hurt your candidacy and may needlessly handicap that of any other aspirant."

Mr. Stevenson remained silent. Either he was not willing to declare himself to me or he was still hesitating about making up his mind.

I continued talking and added: "If you decide to become
a candidate I suggest that you do not allow your name to
be entered in any of the state primaries. Don't waste your
energies. We were able to nominate you in 1952 and we can
do so again in 1956."

But Mr. Stevenson still gave me no indication of what
he intended to do. Some months after our talk he allowed
his name to be entered in the state primaries, and he waged
an exhausting campaign in many parts of the country.

In July, 1956, on my return from Europe, I saw Stevenson again. He came to my room at the Blackstone Hotel,
Room 508, the very same one where in 1944 I had been
called to receive a message from President Roosevelt, who
telephoned me from San Diego to announce that his decision
was that I was to be his running mate in 1944.

This room at the Blackstone has since been my headquarters whenever I visit Chicago. On this July day in 1956,
I had been telling Adlai Stevenson of my trip to Europe. I
related some of my talks with statesmen there and advised
him that, if he were nominated as it appeared certain he
would be, then his big task would be to concentrate on the
peace issue in his campaign against President Eisenhower.

As we talked about some of the major domestic issues,
Stevenson's only comment was: "What is it I am doing
wrong?"

I walked over to the window and, looking down, saw
a man standing at the hotel entrance. I beckoned to Stevenson and then, pointing below, said: "The thing you have got
to do is to learn how to reach that man."

I was trying, as gently as I could, to tell this man—so
gifted in speech and intellect and yet so apparently uncer-

tain of himself and remote from people—that he had to learn how to communicate with the man in the street.

When we parted that day in 1956, I had the feeling that I had failed in my effort to help him. I realized more than ever not only that Stevenson had a problem of making himself understood by the man in the street but that his indecisiveness, unless overcome, would make him ineffectual as a President.

I HAD great expectations for Governor Stevenson. When I first sent for him in 1951 and we met at Blair House, I offered to support him as candidate for the Presidency. Stevenson was making a fine record as governor of Illinois, after waging an effective campaign and winning by a majority of more than half a million.

Stevenson said that he had an obligation to the people of Illinois to run again for governor so that he could complete the program he had initiated. I thought it strange at the time that he would reject a call to party leadership and service to the nation at so critical a moment in history.

I asked Stevenson to come to see me a month later, and again asked him to become a candidate, but again he refused. After another month, I tried still once more by sending the chairman of the party to see him and urge him to reconsider. But Governor Stevenson told Chairman McKinney that he would not run under any circumstances.

I had of course been hoping that we would be able to find, among the rising younger Democrats, a new leadership, and the governor of Illinois was the best prospect in sight when I decided not to run for re-election. At that time we had no idea that the Republicans would nominate a soldier who was a war hero. We thought that the Republicans would nominate Senator Taft or some other conservative, and that it would not be difficult to elect a new Democratic figure for President. Therefore I was very disheartened by Stevenson's reluctant attitude.

I thereupon called in Vice President Barkley to discuss the situation. The Vice President knew my plans and had been present with me on the second occasion I had proposed to Stevenson that he run for the nomination. Barkley had also heard me instruct Chairman McKinney to make one final effort with Governor Stevenson. But now, after three refusals by Stevenson, and with time running short before the convention, I turned to this best known and most beloved Democratic figure, Alben Barkley, and asked him if he would be the candidate. For many reasons, and by right of distinguished service, Barkley was well deserving of consideration and fully qualified. He agreed to have his name submitted to the convention.

But Barkley's candidacy ran into trouble right from the start. The Vice President's personal advisers and representatives mishandled the situation in Chicago. Negotiations with representatives of organized labor were conducted in a manner which led to a misunderstanding and a split in organized labor's support of Barkley. His failure to get labor's full endorsement deeply hurt Barkley, who was a friend of labor, and prompted him to announce his withdrawal the day the convention opened.

Then out of the clear, on the day when the Presidential candidate was to be nominated, Governor Stevenson telephoned me at the White House. He said his friends wanted to nominate him for President. "Would you object," he asked, "if I agreed to run?"

Well, I blew up. I talked to him in language I think he had never heard before. I told him that for months I had been trying to get him to be the candidate. Now, at the last possible moment, he had changed his mind. But he was at that time the best prospect we had and I said I would support him.

On Sunday, the day before the convention opened, the caucus of the Illinois delegation met. Stevenson was present. At this caucus the Governor *still* withheld his permission to allow the delegation to place his name in nomination. But the chairman of the caucus declared that if another state placed the name of Stevenson before the convention, Illinois would feel itself bound to second that nomination. I was informed that the Governor remained silent at this statement but did not at this point discourage the Illinois delegation with instructions *not* to nominate him. Thus, characteristically by indirection, Stevenson became an active candidate.

When the convention opened, a deadlock developed. I thereupon boarded a plane for Chicago to take a hand. If I had not flown to Chicago from Washington, Stevenson would not have been nominated.

I got the leaders of the convention to confer with me immediately on my arrival and told them that I regarded Stevenson as the logical candidate. As a result, Stevenson was nominated.

Stevenson's difficulty in getting the nomination would not have developed if he had indicated long enough in advance that he would be willing to run. Some of Stevenson's supporters anticipated that he would be drafted, but a draft could not and would not have materialized at that convention. A draft rarely can be worked on a convention. It required the intervention of the President to get Stevenson through.

Then Stevenson went out and conducted a campaign that was not in support of the Democratic program of President Roosevelt and myself. You cannot successfully run as a Democrat, with a Democratic administration in power, without running on the record of the administration.

IN 1956, when Stevenson finally made up his mind to run a second time, I would have wished that some other national figures might have come to the fore. Yet I was prepared to support him again. But some of Stevenson's actions and statements that year aroused further doubts in my mind about his dimensions as a leader and as a potential President.

I did not like the hesitating and vacillating policy of the Eisenhower Administration and the damage it was doing to the country. I thought the Democrats ought to give the country a better choice by offering it a man of decision.

A speech of Stevenson's earlier in 1956 left me uneasy. In that speech, it seemed to me that he did not fully grasp the implications and the danger of the proposal he made. That proposal was that we unilaterally stop the testing of the hydrogen explosions.

Obviously, Stevenson meant well. But I thought that he got on to a subject with which he was not fully familiar. He should have gotten all the facts that could have been available to him before speaking, or he should at least have realized that the world did not know what the Russians were doing in developing nuclear weapons. And what is even more to the point, the hydrogen bomb is not a political issue. The dangers of fall-out are a problem for all people everywhere and should not be made a subject of partisan politics. American national policy, whether under a Democratic or Republican administration, is to put an immediate halt to the making and testing of all nuclear weapons *under an international system of control and inspection* so that security and peace can be effectively maintained throughout the world. The Russians have persistently prevented any agreement or set-up by which the world might be guaranteed protection from nuclear explosions and nuclear competition.

We now know that when some people were advocating in 1956 that the American government stop its tests of the hydrogen bomb, the Russians were already in possession of a multimegaton stockpile of intermediate ballistic missiles with thermonuclear warheads. At that time, the United States had just started to build up its own stockpile.

At the time, I thought it would have been more prudent for Stevenson to ascertain other critical aspects of the nuclear problem outside the scope of science. His advocacy of unilateral cessation of nuclear testing was not only bad politics but revealed Stevenson's lack of comprehension of all the implications of this critical issue. This distressed me.

But it was evident that Stevenson could carry the convention, and I was prepared to contribute to party unity even though I did not approve of what some of the leaders of the national committee supporting Stevenson were trying to do. I like an open convention, and even encouraged an open convention in 1948 when I could, as President, have arranged for a closed convention.

I BEGAN to see signs long before the 1956 convention that Stevenson apparently was still embarrassed by this farmer from Missouri. Therefore, I gave some thought to what I could do to make it easier for Stevenson to disassociate himself from me politically.

I knew I would have to do something drastic. It did not matter whether people would get abusive about my move. I had never hesitated to do the things I thought necessary, regardless of whether they were popular or not. My reputation, whatever it was, was made or unmade long before that. If I ever was embarrassed, I embarrassed myself. And I did not mind it.

As a first move in that direction, I began to consider endorsing some other candidate. I decided on Governor Harriman of New York. His record in many years of service to the country in various capacities from ambassador to Cabinet officer, and his unflinching loyalty to the New Deal and Fair Deal, entitled him to be taken seriously as a Presidential candidate. I realized that, in all fairness to Harriman, I had to point out to him that he would have difficulties, almost insurmountable, in getting this convention to nominate him. The convention was pretty much a cut-and-dried affair for Stevenson. Harriman, deserving as he was, could only be a long shot, even if there were hope of making the convention an open one.

I called a press conference shortly after my arrival in Chicago for the convention. I announced that I would support the candidacy of Averell Harriman. I said I believed he would make a good President.

This came as a thunderbolt to the supporters of Stevenson. I had opened up a political hornet's nest. Emotions ran high, and many self-appointed liberal custodians of the party did not spare invective. Some even questioned, at this late stage, the liberalism of the former President. There was even a suggestion that my days of usefulness in Democratic politics were over and that I would, henceforth, be consigned to permanent oblivion.

Some critics charged that I had lost all political judgment and sense when I followed up my endorsement of Harriman with the prediction that Stevenson could not possibly be elected. I said that if Stevenson were nominated by the Democratic convention he would carry fewer states than he did in 1952. I based my statement on the fact that he lost by such a tremendous majority in the 1952 campaign and that he did not undertake the campaign with a complete endorsement by him of the Democratic party and its principles.

I could understand the abuse and the anger that was aimed at me, and I was not bothered. After all, I had been through similar periods before. It was a little hard on some of my friends.

One thing was certain. Any ties that Stevenson thought he had with me, or thought it expedient to have with me, were now effectively severed. Any political liability he fancied I represented to his cause was now removed.

Of course, when the convention nominated Stevenson, I

took the floor to announce that, as a loyal Democrat, I would do everything the party wanted me to do in the campaign on behalf of the candidate. And in the campaign that followed, I undertook one of the most exhausting schedules of personal appearances I had ever assumed, and I was just as unsparing of myself as if I were campaigning for myself.

This is the way I think a man must act in politics. He must close ranks and forget personalities. This is the very heart of our Republic—to debate the issues as vigorously as we can and then, after the people have spoken, carry on and work together.

A lesson all candidates should remember is that you cannot turn your back on your party's record. You can improve it but you cannot deal with the future without tying in to the past. The past of the Democratic party under the New Deal and the Fair Deal represents some of the most important historic advances in the life of this Republic. And the last man in the world to ignore it should be the nominee of that party.

5

At Home with People

A MAN who has been in the position that I was is always a subject for gossip. That is why, when we resettled in Independence, we found it difficult to get domestic help —help that would, as my mother used to say, "keep their mouths shut when they ought to."

We are of the old-fashioned cult that believes in home privacy, and we would much rather do the things that need to be done in the home ourselves than have someone around who will go out and gossip about it.

Most of the people who worked for us before we went to the White House were no longer physically able to do steady work when we returned home. But we get along reasonably well. We have two or three people come in once or twice a week to clean up and help Mrs. Truman get things arranged so that the house runs almost exactly as it used to.

Mrs. Truman is a good cook. She has always been a good cook, but she protests she is not. You will find some of her recipes in national cook books. Every member of my family, from my grandmothers on both sides of the house all the way down, have been good cooks. Of course, Mrs. Truman has been very careful about my waistline because she fears it might have a bad effect on my heart. I think that is something the doctors told her.

For breakfast I usually have toast and bacon and maybe a soft-boiled egg, or poached egg, or scrambled eggs. Bess has about the same thing. She regularly has coffee, and sometimes I have a cup of coffee with her—but mostly I have no drink at all for breakfast, except milk or water or sometimes hot tea.

When people ask me what my favorite foods are, I say that, among others, I am very fond of roast beef. I prefer the cut next to the end piece, or the outside cut. I do not like rare or raw meat of any kind. And I like baked potatoes!

I am typical of the Midwest in my food preferences. Most midwesterners serve their beef well done, rather than rare, as they do in the East. The reason is probably that the Midwest furnishes most of the beef for the nation, and some of the early settlers of the Midwest were of the opinion that only coyotes and predatory animals ate raw beef. Anyway, that is the reason why I, for one, like my meat well cooked.

Incidentally, I do not like to hunt animals, and I never have. I do not believe in shooting at anything that cannot shoot back.

I am very fond of bacon, ham, sausage, and things of that sort. We usually have bacon or sausage for breakfast, not together, but time about.

I have never fussed too much about food. I eat what I like and pass up what I do not. I never complain. When I was in the army, as commanding officer of a battery, one of my staff kicked about the food. I put him in the kitchen to take charge and see what he could do. I think that is the proper way to deal with critics.

Since our daughter Margaret went to New York to live, originally to pursue her singing and acting career and later because of her marriage, Mrs. Truman and I have been living alone in Independence in a fourteen-room house on Delaware Street. This is the house where we lived for many years before going to Washington. It is over a hundred years old, and had been in my wife's family for several generations. Sometimes it pops and cracks as it keeps settling, and we have had to prop it up with steel beams.

I had expected to rebuild the old farm house out at Grandview, Missouri, as it was when my grandfather and grandmother lived there. This was the home of both my grandfathers, as well as of my mother and father. Grandfather Truman came to live with my mother and father there after leaving Lamar, Missouri. But the house stood in the path of the rapidly expanding metropolitan area of Kansas City. There was need for a shopping center in that location. I had also hoped to build a library on forty acres that I had set aside for that purpose, but the idea of rebuilding the house and erecting the library had to be abandoned to make way for the expanding community.

The sale of this land for a shopping center provided some needed economic help to my brother and sister, as well as myself. But since the shopping center has been built on our family farm land, I get a nostalgic feeling every time I pass it. For it was there where I used to sow wheat and harvest it, and there where I helped my father and brother thresh it. It was there that we used to plant corn and gather it in.

It was no longer the old home for me—the home established by my grandfather in 1850. I cannot help but wish that I could have kept that farm as it was in the beginning.

But Mrs. Truman and I decided to stay on Delaware Street in Independence, where we are quite comfortable. We have a large back yard and a front lawn, and the green reminds us of the farm. Two years after our return from Washington, we made necessary repairs to the interior of the house and did some modernizing.

When I get up at about five to five-thirty in the morning, I go downstairs and do a round of work in the house. In the wintertime, this used to include tending the furnace and carrying out the ashes—that is, until gas was put in and made me give it up. Sometimes I try to take care of other household chores, which Mrs. Truman has been trying to keep me from doing. She runs the house.

There was one chore she did ask me to do, which I wanted to get out of doing. That was to mow the lawn. I think she did this mainly to tease me a little. She takes great pride in the yard and puts in many hours tending the rose garden. We do call in outside help to tend to the grounds and trees and the cutting of the grass. But one weekend Mrs. Truman said that I had done nothing about the lawn. So I waited till Sunday morning, just as our neighbors were beginning to pass on their way to church, and I took out the lawn mower and started to cut the grass. Mrs. Truman, preparing to leave for church, was horrified to see me cutting the lawn.

"What are you doing on Sunday?" she asked.

"I'm doing what you asked me to do," I replied.

Meanwhile the neighbors continued to pass by the

house. Their glances were not lost on Mrs. Truman. She never asked me to mow the lawn again.

As part of my daily routine, I usually take a walk of a mile and a half, at a pace of 120 steps a minute, from six-thirty to seven each morning. Mrs. Truman generally comes downstairs about seven to seven-fifteen to get our breakfast. Until breakfast is ready, I read the newspapers and such mail as is delivered to the house instead of to the office. At breakfast, Mrs. Truman and I discuss the things that have to be done in the house and on the grounds and the people who will be coming to do the work.

I used to walk to the Library, a distance of six blocks, but soon had to stop that because too many people wanted to talk to me along the way and I could not get to my office on time. On that walk, too, I went at a pace of 120 steps a minute. I learned to do this during my period of service in the National Guard and in the First World War.

I still walk at that pace, not because I wish to hurry but because, if you are going to take a walk for your physical benefit, it is necessary that you walk as if you are going some place. If you walk 120 paces a minute, your whole body gets a vigorous workout. You swing your arms and take deep breaths as you walk.

After you are fifty years old, this is the best exercise you can take. Of course, some aging exhibitionists try to prove that they can play tennis or handball or anything else they did when they were eighteen. And every once in a while one of them falls dead of a heart attack. I say that's not for me.

After breakfast I drive to the Library, getting there long before any of the secretarial staff. This is usually shortly before eight o'clock. Miss Rose Conway, who was my confidential secretary at the White House, continued in that capacity when I settled down to my office routine. She came back to Kansas City to head up my office at the Federal Reserve Bank Building, where I first set up facilities to receive people and house my staff and to wait for the completion of the Truman Library. I remained at the office in the Federal Reserve Bank Building for over three years, and it was there that I planned and wrote my Memoirs. Miss Conway has always been meticulous in observing confidences; she has, to an exceptional degree, the Missouri sense of reticence and discretion.

While I was in the White House, and even afterwards, there were many distorted reports in the press about how some people betrayed my trust and broke my confidence. The fact is that such betrayals were very few. It is to be expected that, when a person is close to the Chief Executive, all sorts of people will importune him to tell what is going on behind the scenes. Sometimes a person in that position cannot resist the temptation to break over. Considering everything, I was fortunate that there was so little breach of faith.

I had to keep my past experience in mind when I began writing my Memoirs, and I had to select a staff of researchers who were not only competent but trustworthy. I soon found out that "Potomac Fever" is not peculiar to Washington, and that even researchers assigned to simple and temporary duties, such as checking data, can soon develop surprising airs. I should not have been surprised at what some people will do when they get into proximity with the person of even a former President. However, it all worked out for the best.

Recently, some of my friends have asked me whether I would ever want to return to Washington to live. I tell them I have had all of Washington that I want. I never had the complex of being a big shot, be it in Washington proper or in Virginia or in Maryland, though all of them have their attractions. I like going to Washington for visits, but I prefer my life in Missouri and I prefer to live the way I do.

WHEREVER I go, I try to see as many people as I can. And people come to see me from all parts of the world. They often ask me how it is that I came to express myself so vigorously on problems that have to do with minority groups in our country. The questions sometimes imply that perhaps my motives were political. Those who can remember my campaign in 1948 for civil rights would know better than to ask that kind of question. The plain fact is that early in life I was impressed by the plight of some minority groups, long before I thought of politics. While still a boy, I was witness to some of their miseries.

For example, I can never forget the look on the faces of Negroes I saw in flight from a burning cross in Independence. To put it mildly, I violently disapproved of the Ku Klux Klan then as I do now. And I learned very early of the lot of the underpaid wage earner. The privations of these people left a deep impression on me. When I was approaching college age, I had to go to work because my father could not afford to send me to college. I started working as timekeeper on the Santa Fe for a contractor and later at a bank for thirty-five dollars a month. I found out how even bank employees were underpaid and how they were treated and what they thought about it.

When I went back to the farm, on leaving my job at the bank, I got to know a lot of farm hands who came out of the little towns close to us. Their usual wage at that time was ten cents an hour, or a dollar twenty cents a day for a twelve-hour day. My father and my brother and I always increased the wages of the men who worked for us—giving them anywhere from one dollar and fifty cents to two dollars a day and their meals. These farm workers were of the best stock that the country produced—hard working, upright and good citizens. Yet they had to live almost in poverty. In the face of all that, most of them managed somehow to get along, raise a good family and even send some of their sons to college.

I have a special sympathy for the fellow who does not have the advantages of those who belong to the so-called topnotch social outfits and privileged groups. And I have never lost sight of their problems. I am sorry to see a growth of snobbery in the United States in recent years. I especially deplore the tendency to look down on people who work with their hands.

I suppose we will always have some snobbery in the world, and that is too bad. I do not think any man should be ashamed of what he does, no matter what it is, so long as it is useful and honorable. The man who is proud of his job has no trouble in this free country of ours, and I do not believe in anyone's taking the attitude that he is better than anyone else because he apparently has a better job.

I like to think that in this country a man who makes good on one job can always expect promotion to a better one, and I hope that will always be so. I would like to see our youngsters grow up with an outlook that they must not, under any circumstances, feel that they are any better than the other fellow because they have a better financial status in the community.

It has always been the case that people who live in big houses think that they are better than those who live in small houses. I never thought so, and I guess that is one of the reasons I feel I had little trouble making the people understand what I believe about our kind of freedom and democracy.

6

I Survive
Major Surgery

I WAS fortunate to come through the ordeal of close to eight years at the White House without damage to my physical condition. In normal times, the office of the Presidency imposes enormous strains on the physical resources of the person of the Chief Executive. But in times of national emergencies, the weight of responsibility becomes almost unbearable.

My doctor thought it astonishing that I was able to return home so well and fit, and so eager to get to work at something without wanting to take any rest, and, in fact, not really needing any kind of holiday. When I did go with my family to Hawaii, shortly after my return to Independence, I soon found myself restless. I felt I was wasting time. I had never been accustomed to the luxury of leisure before, and this was no life for me, especially when I felt fit and eager to get back to work.

I had been able to meet the ceaseless demands of the

Presidency without interruption, except for the few days I had to spend in the Walter Reed Hospital due to an intestinal cold toward the end of my last year in office.

Even while at Walter Reed, I attended to all necessary official business, although the doctors tried to discourage it. And the doctors liked it even less when I decided to get up and out of bed and go out for a walk. I was warned that there were indications that my lungs were accumulating fluid which might bring on a dangerous congestion. But I had the feeling that I could "walk this fluid off," since there was no appreciable rise in my temperature, and I had always found my walks so beneficial to me. I returned from this walk feeling much better, and I left the hospital for the White House shortly thereafter.

I had been brought up in the simple tradition not to fuss too much about myself physically and to give the body a chance to act naturally so that it can take care of itself in its own way. But this does not mean that I think doctors are unnecessary. It is just that I am against coddling myself. Whenever any member of our family has been threatened with any kind of serious illness, we have never hesitated to send for the family doctor, and he has always been a man in whom we have confidence. As a matter of fact, early in my career in public life, I adopted the attitude toward health of the ancient Chinese, who said that doctors should be paid to keep you well, since they so wisely assumed that prevention is more important than cure.

When I became judge of Jackson County, after serving in the First World War, I began getting regular physical check-ups by going to Hot Springs, Arkansas, to the Army and Navy Hospital, where twice a year I had myself checked from the crown of my head to the tips of my toes. I kept up this practice even after I went to Washington as the junior United States Senator from Missouri.

I knew, early in life, that I had a slow heartbeat, but I never let it worry me. In fact, I was told by our family doctor that this slow heartbeat was preferable to a fast beat, and could contribute to a longer life.

I was blessed with the wonderful gift of good health by my forebears, on both sides of the family. They all lived to a ripe old age, and there was not a single hypochondriac among them. All of us have had our share of minor upsets, from time to time. But we always try to let nature work things out, and we have not let every little ailment upset us.

Against such a background, it was not surprising, then, that I was able to go through three score and fifteen years of life, embracing war, politics, the Presidency, and even retirement, with only two serious illnesses.

THE first serious illness I had was diphtheria, which I contracted when I was eight years old. In those days, the only applied remedy for diphtheria was half a tumbler of whisky. The whisky was administered for the purpose of "making you retch your sickness away." I have never forgotten that first swallow of whisky that was poured into me when I came down with diphtheria.

The taste of the whisky was bad. And the smell was awful. To this day I still hate the smell of whisky, and I do not like the taste of it. As a matter of fact, I never drank whisky or any alcoholic beverage from the time I had diphtheria until twenty-six years later when I was thirty-four years old. I was then serving in the First World War with my battery in France with the AEF.

Because of the dangers of contamination in the water areas, the water was so heavily chlorinated that we could not stomach it. We drank wine instead. And from time to time, we supplemented it with cognac. I liked the taste of wine, and today I may take white wine with my meals when I dine out. I especially like Barsac and Sauternes. Red wines are pleasing, but I do not care too much for them.

Although I still do not like the smell or taste of whisky, I do take on the average of two ounces of bourbon a day, usually drinking it before meals. It is necessary for me to use this amount of bourbon to improve my circulation because of my chronic low blood pressure.

And while this may seem unusually revealing about the personal tastes and habits of a contrary and taciturn Missourian, I realize that I have lost some of my rights to privacy. So I may as well answer other questions about what I do or don't do—as, for example, whether I smoke.

I have never smoked, not because of any special virtue on my part, but my father never smoked, and my father's father never smoked, and it happened that neither my brother nor I ever got interested in smoking. My brother and I did try smoking cornsilk, as every boy on a farm does some time or other, but we never liked it. Only once did I attempt to puff on a cigar. It made me so sick I never tried it again.

I AM inclined to attribute my good health, and that of my family, primarily to our outlook on life, and to our philosophical approach to other people and to ourselves.

I grew up to look for the good in people. I have never regarded people with suspicion—for such an attitude usually leads to worrying yourself into being a pessimist about everything, people included. I have always tried to give a person the benefit of the doubt. That is why I take the position that a fellow has to go wrong in fact before I condemn him.

Now, my mother used to call our family the "touch-me-not family" because we did not welcome intrusion on our private family affairs. But we always have had an interest in doing everything we could to help other people whenever they were in trouble or in need. I had grandfathers on both sides who were as tough-minded as could be—yet they never passed up a chance to help their neighbors.

Then I also developed the habit, very early in life, of not worrying about any situation that I could not do anything about. I would always try to find the solution to a problem I faced, and if I found the solution I did something about it right away.

Sleep is the best antidote for worry, and it gives the human machine a chance to rehabilitate itself. It is tough to turn off the mind sometimes, but unless you learn to do it, you will not be able to get the sleep you need. And I have never forced myself to think when my energy was low. I simply will not tackle a problem involving an important decision until I feel completely relaxed.

All this accounts, in some measure, for the fact that looking after my physical well-being in the White House did not tax the full time and energies of my able White House

physician, Major General Wallace H. Graham. Dr. Graham
saw me every day, and made sure that I had periodic check-
ups. He is the son of my old family doctor and has been a
friend of the family for many years.

The medical education of the younger Graham was
more extensive and included attendance at some of the leading medical schools in Europe. While in the White House,
Dr. Graham was able to treat members of my staff and their
families, as well as some of the White House police force and
some of the Secret Service assigned to White House duty. He
gave of himself unsparingly and, in addition to his long
schedule of appointments, he volunteered his services as a
surgeon at the Walter Reed Hospital.

When I returned to Independence, Dr. Graham moved
back to Kansas City to join his father in the general practice
of medicine and surgery. I was glad, of course, to have him
back here so that he could continue to look after my family
and see that we continued our check-ups.

ALL was going well, as I kept busy working on my Memoirs
while trying to meet all the new and unexpected demands
on me for appearances in all parts of the country. But one
evening, in the summer of 1954 while attending a performance of "Call Me Madam" at the open air theatre in Swope
Park, I suddenly had a violent seizure and lost my food.

Mrs. Truman immediately helped me to our car and
took the wheel to drive back to Independence. She had to
stop several times on the way home as I found it increasingly
difficult to hold anything down. Dr. Graham was sent for

and, upon examination, found that I had suffered a severe gall bladder attack.

I was taken to the Research Hospital in Kansas City the following morning. The gall bladder attack was similar in nature to the one I had experienced in 1940, but more painful. In 1940, a doctor in Washington had diagnosed the complaint as gall bladder trouble. At that time, the pain passed quickly and I paid no further attention to the possibility that there was anything seriously wrong. And for fourteen years there had been no further sign of disturbance in that area until that evening in Swope Park in Kansas City.

On the way to the hospital, I was told that I would probably have to undergo surgery. I thereupon took out my briefcase, which I had taken along with me in anticipation of reading some important correspondence, and took from it a pad of paper. On this pad I wrote out a codicil to my will.

I had intended to reassign a twenty-acre plot of farm land adjoining the family farm, which I had especially acquired as a site for a library to which I could turn over my papers for study and research by students and historians. The city of Independence had voted shortly before to dedicate an ideally situated city park for that project. It was a generous and gracious act by the citizens of my home town, and I felt honored and pleased.

Despite the fact that I was in some discomfort and had to write in a moving automobile, my attorney, Judge Samuel I. Rosenman, told me later that the codicil turned out to be a pretty good document and would have stood up legally. But he rewrote it later anyway, when there were new developments in the affairs of my family and I wanted to make provisions to deal with them.

After my arrival at the hospital, I went through a series of tests which confirmed the need for surgery. The following morning, my gall bladder was removed, and while the surgeons were at it they found my appendix was infected and inflamed and also had to go. The doctors looked for signs of other possible trouble, including malignancy, which doctors tell me is a matter of routine in the course of such surgery. And it is always welcome news when doctors inform you they have found no trace of malignancy.

The operation was pronounced a success, and when I came out of the anesthesia, I felt no special discomfort in having been through my first experience with surgery. I was reasonably cheerful—but I have never taken too kindly to being subjected to medical restrictions. I submitted to "doctor's orders" without too much resistance.

No sooner had the news of my operation reached the public than there followed a situation and a reaction for which my family and I were totally unprepared. Nor could the hospital have anticipated what was to come. A concern about my condition suddenly developed throughout the country, and there descended upon the hospital a steady stream of newspaper and press association reporters, radio and television people and newsreel cameramen. News headquarters were set up at the hospital on a twenty-four hour basis, with all the necessary facilities and equipment, imposing a great burden on hospital communications and personnel.

People in town and by long distance began to telephone the hospital at all hours, paralyzing the switchboard facilities.

People came individually and in groups to make personal inquiries about my condition, and many came to offer prayers. I was especially touched by a cable from Moscow informing me that the Russian Baptists there were praying for my recovery. Thousands of get-well cards, letters, messages and telegrams were arriving at the hospital and at my office, including cables from abroad. The messages were not only from my friends, and a great many people I did not know, but from officials and heads of government.

I was astonished at this expression of concern. I was deeply touched and moved by it. I could not understand why, as a private citizen, I should still arouse such widespread interest. I kept forgetting that, having once been where I was, I could never expect to cut myself off from public attention.

Since leaving Washington, I had resolved to answer as many communications from people as I could manage with the small staff I had. When I was informed of the flood of messages that were arriving, I was troubled about how I could ever tell all these kind people that I had actually received their messages and how grateful I was for their thoughtfulness.

THAT summer of 1954 was abnormally hot in Kansas City, and the thermometer outside the hospital windows ranged between 110 and 114 by mid-afternoon. Mrs. Truman was at my side constantly, and she read the newspapers to me, as well as current magazines and many of the letters and messages that came in.

I did not realize how punishing the heat was to the other patients and visitors to the hospital, which was without air conditioning. I do not mind the heat, and I have never cared for air conditioning for myself, preferring fresh air no matter how hot or cold.

When the director of the Research Hospital wanted to put in an air conditioner in my room I declined. The director tried to insist, because he said it seemed to him that I was showing signs of being affected by the unusually intense heat. But I felt that, despite the good intention of the hospital to provide me with every comfort, I should not be given special privileges, since no one else in the hospital was provided with air conditioning.

But several days later, an old friend of mine who had been sitting outside my hospital door from morning to evening, sent word that he wanted to see me about something important. The doctor had ordered, as a precautionary measure, that no visitors be admitted.

But I asked the doctor to allow my friend in for a few minutes. After inquiring how I felt, he said: "It may be all right for you to do without air conditioning, but what about Mrs. Truman sitting here day after day in this insufferable heat? Why are you being so stubborn, and why don't you let the hospital put air conditioning in?"

I sent for the hospital superintendent, Robert Adams, who had been wonderfully considerate in anticipating all my needs, and asked if he would stop by to see me on his next round. He came at once. And within the hour, an air conditioning unit was installed.

My convalescence was at this time progressing normally, and the doctors even thought I was responding to treatment exceptionally well. To prevent complications, the doctors had prescribed certain antibiotics. Suddenly I was assailed by internal and external hives and found myself in acute discomfort.

The doctors described this condition as a bizarre reaction to the antibiotics which had been administered, informing me that such a reaction occurs rarely. I was no longer able to take food by mouth and had to be fed intravenously. Everything seemed to be going wrong all at once, and it was apparent that things were taking a turn for the worse.

Dr. Graham naturally became alarmed and called in three specialists for consultation. When news got out that my condition was becoming unfavorable, a number of leading specialists from different parts of the country sent word that they were standing by if needed by Dr. Graham. Several even telephoned to say that they were all packed and ready to fly to Kansas City at once.

I knew that I was not in the best possible shape, and I understood that the doctors were worried. But I felt confident that I would come through. The doctors were taking all necessary medical steps and were doing everything possible to combat the complications that had set in.

One afternoon, when I saw that I was not getting better and was feeling very weak because I had not been retaining much nourishment, I asked the doctor in attendance whether there could be any harm in my having a soft-boiled egg. Pausing to think about it, the doctor said he had no objection if I thought I could handle it. I sensed that he had some doubt that I could.

I asked the nurse on duty to get me a soft-boiled egg

and bring it in a white cup. The nurse seemed a bit taken aback and said: "Why a white cup?"

I whispered, in a feeble attempt to be good-humored, "So that I'll know it's clean."

I think she understood I was trying to do something for myself on a sort of hunch I had. I got my egg, and I got my white cup, and I ate the egg—all of it—and for the first time since the reaction to the antibiotics had set in, I took nourishment by mouth—and retained it.

The combination of expert medical care and special attention from the hospital staff and nurses, together with my naturally tough physical constitution, began to pull me back to health. And I depended so much upon the daily presence of Mrs. Truman.

Antibiotics have done wonderful things in combating many diseases, and have rightly been called miracle drugs. But I don't think some antibiotics and I get along too well.

I RETURNED to my home in Independence, remembering the many kindnesses of the Research Hospital staff. The board of trustees of the hospital did an unusual thing after I left the hospital, sending director Robert Adams to my home with a bill covering all expenses and hospital fees marked, "Paid in Full." This was a gracious act, and I was deeply touched by it. But I told Mr. Adams that I insisted on paying the bill and that I hoped the board of trustees of the Research Hospital would understand the reason why I wanted to do this and how genuinely grateful I was. I have always preferred to be treated as any other individual.

It took me only a few months to get back to my normal condition, although I had been told it would take a year to achieve full recovery. I have been feeling fine ever since and, as a matter of fact, I have been doing more work than I had done at any time since leaving the White House. I have put in longer hours, have done more writing and made more frequent trips, both in the interest of politics and to lecture before the young people at colleges and universities.

I continue to work six days a week, and often on Sunday when at home. I devote many hours to my work at the Library, reading the mail, dictating, conferring and instructing my secretary as to what I want done during the week.

All this has proved that I can get along without my gall bladder. I have never indulged myself with fancy foods. I have always eaten simply and in small quantities and at reasonably regular hours. But now and then I do miss certain foods, such as salted nuts, that the doctors advised me to leave alone. Once in a while I cross them up, only to find that it is myself I am crossing up.

7

Should a Former
President Speak
His Mind?

As a private citizen, I had hoped to be able to talk as
freely as any private citizen is entitled to speak, or at
least as freely as some people thought I did as President.
But I had to adjust myself soon after returning home to the
fact that I had to be very careful about what I said publicly,
and sometimes even privately, on any subject, be it how to
bring up children or what to do about Russia.

When a former President speaks, people continue to
pay attention to what he has to say, even if they pay no attention to the advice he gives. This I can understand. People
regard advice as one of the cheapest commodities in the
world, especially on politics, and particularly from one who
is no longer supposed to have any influence in politics. A
former President cannot expect to have the same political

leverage that he had in the White House. And that is as it ought to be.

As President, I had sought a united front and the elimination of partisan politics in the conduct of our foreign affairs. Politicking in that area can only mislead and damage our relations with our allies and provide propaganda for the Communists. Therefore, as a private citizen, I wanted to go on doing all I could to discourage narrow partisan debate on foreign policy. But when people, here and abroad, began to seek my views on international developments, I had to consider what effect my statements would have on the Administration's handling of foreign policy.

Two world wars had brought about great changes in our position as a nation. Many profound developments, growing out of that position, took place during my Administration. The change to a Republican administration, after twenty years of Democratic control of the government, whatever the expressed wishes of the people at the polls may have been, could not materially alter the course on which we were set. We had assumed the burden of responsibility for maintaining peace. Any interruption of our role as a leader of the free world could only spell trouble for us and for our allies.

Since I left the White House, events have proved that the course was right. The fact is that the basic foreign policy of the United States is deeply rooted in our history and geography and is of a continuing nature, no matter what President or which political party happens to be in control of the White House.

The world in which we live leaves little room for anyone in a position of responsibility ever again to give a serious thought to any form of isolationism. Historically, I do not believe that we have ever been completely withdrawn from the world in isolation, and the few attempts in the past to impose isolationism on us resulted in tragedy. The most tragic instance, I think, was our decision to reject the League of Nations, which contributed to the conditions that brought about the Second World War.

We have a tendency to label certain of our foreign policy pronouncements as doctrines and attach to them the names of their authors, such as the Monroe Doctrine. I think this overlooks the essential point that these pronouncements are not so much personal declarations of individuals as they are the expression of a continuing and fundamental American policy. American policy has always been to further the security and the welfare of the nation and to contribute to the preservation of world peace.

I have always held that our action in Greece and Turkey, labeled the Truman Doctrine, is just a continuation of basic American policy.

During the early days of the Eisenhower Administration, it was most trying for me to restrain myself from making the comments I wanted to make when the President took certain actions and made certain statements. I thought they were badly advised—such as the "unleashing" of Chiang Kai-shek. These actions by the new Administration had obvious political overtones and were in direct conflict with our basic position in the Pacific.

I HAVE often deplored the waste of the experience and skill of men who have served in important positions in government, only to have them lost to the country because of shifts in political control. The British have a better way of making use of many of their experienced men out of government, whatever their politics. In England they have a Privy Council, among whose members are former Prime Ministers and Cabinet ministers. The Privy Council is called upon from time to time to advise the government in major policy matters. In this way the British are able to maintain continuity of government—especially continuity of their foreign policy.

Of course, the British can do this easily, because they do not carry their personalities into their political contests. When elections are over there is no personal bitterness left over. I think we ought to establish something similar here. We could not only utilize a great store of valuable experience and judgment but also help achieve what I consider our greatest need, and that is continuity of our basic foreign policy.

There should be no room nor any reason for personal bitterness either during or after our political campaigns and elections. I never had any bitter feelings about my opponents, and was just as friendly with the opposition after elections. Some of my campaigns were pretty bitter, but when they were over my opponents were always welcome in my office and I was glad to see them any time they wanted to talk to me. They were always courteously treated, and sometimes they were helpful.

As a matter of fact, I never did go into personalities in any of my campaigns. In most of my campaigns, I found it best not to mention my opponent by name because, by doing so, it just gave him a chance to get into the headlines.

And as President, I appointed many outstanding Republicans to high places in the government. For example, there were Republicans in my Cabinet. When it came to foreign policy, politics were completely out. Defense was another department where we looked for the man first and hardly ever at the political affiliation of the man. When one of my executive assistants, on one occasion, made a point of telling me that a man I was about to appoint to an important post was a Republican, I said: "You find the best man so that we can do the best job, and leave the politics to me."

THESE were the thoughts that were in my mind when I was asked to comment publicly on some of the decisions of the new Administration, especially on foreign policy. But I felt that I could not indulge in the privilege of my newly restored freedoms as a private citizen. I realized, too, that I had a continuing responsibility. And I was determined to do nothing to embarrass the President and his conduct of foreign policy. Whenever I did find it necessary to give my views on foreign policy, I tried to do so in a constructive way. I could not lend myself to any purely partisan politics in this field.

I believe, too, that under our system the functioning of government is a continuing process in domestic as well as in foreign affairs. It was for this reason that I had taken unprecedented steps to arrange for an orderly turnover of every department of the government to the incoming Administration. Immediately after the election, I had put into motion the vast machinery of government to brief and to inform the representatives of the President-designate on the operations and the up-to-the-minute transactions of my Administration.

I have been asked what the new Eisenhower Administration was hoping to accomplish by devoting so much time, from the very outset, to an attempt to discredit the previous Administration. I thought it was the work of amateurs in politics. It would have been much better for the country and the world if the people in charge of the new Administration had directed their energies to running the government and making only such changes in its operations as they deemed wise and necessary.

In these times, a new administration should weigh carefully the reversal of any policy of the previous administration. And once a change is decided on, it ought to be done gradually to avoid any possible serious dislocations. There are times, of course, when the nation is at war or in the throes of an emergency such as the one we faced in the early thirties, and then decisions and actions must be swift.

ONE of the greatest assets of our two-party system, and a reason for its continuance, is that there are people in *both* parties who represent all shades of opinion. When one party takes charge of government in succession to the other, the resulting changeover is not a revolution—as is the case where dictators are in control—but a peaceful orderly process. I do not think it is always in the best interests of the country for a new administration, regardless of its politics, to cut itself off completely and abruptly from a preceding administration. In my judgment, it is in the best interest of the country that policies of previous administrations be followed through and studied for possible improvement and vigorous enforcement.

For example, Democratic administrations have made extensive applications of the anti-trust laws enacted by Republican administrations. And the Eisenhower Administration eventually found that all the social welfare laws put on the statute books by the New Deal and the Fair Deal Administrations were desirable and necessary.

But there is a fundamental difference between the two major parties. That difference lies in how to deal with the social and economic problems of the nation. One party inclines to the belief that leadership should be from the top and that social and economic benefits should filter downward. The other party believes that the power of government should not be in the hands of the select few and that the benefits of our economy should have the widest distribution, beginning at the bottom with the greatest number of people. And I'm sure I do not have to label which of these parties is the Republican and which the Democratic.

I have been fiercely partisan in politics and always militantly liberal. I will be that way as long as I live. Yet I think we would lose something important to our political life if the conservatives were all in one party and the liberals all in the other. This would make us a nation divided either into two opposing and irreconcilable camps or into even smaller and more contentious groups, such as have plagued recent European history.

The existence of liberal and conservative groups in each party provides checks and balances which, in the long run, have served the nation well. Unfortunately, we have too frequently lost badly needed progressive legislation because of a coalition of conservatives of both parties. But such delays have made the people all the more aware of the needed legislation when the issues come up in campaigns at election time. And the people have their say in the matter every two years, at which time Congress gets its mandate. The people need to be aroused about these issues and stimulated by the debates between opposing elements within both political parties.

FOR a man who has never gone to college, it often seems a little surprising to me that I get so many requests to lecture at colleges. What I find more surprising is that, when I talk to people who have gone to college, so many of them have so little understanding of the real nature of our government.

Many seem to think that all there is to government are political campaigns and elections to vote people into office, and that after each election, as one political party goes in and the other political party goes out, the whole process of government starts all over again. The fact is that government never ceases to function—even when a President dies. It is an ever-continuing process. We would have chaos if every time there was an election there was a complete break with all that had just gone before.

The United States Senate is the best example of how the founding fathers planned for continuity in government. The Constitution provides that a third of the membership of the Senate be selected every two years. Each senator is elected for a term of six years so that, as two-thirds of the senators remain, the Senate becomes a continuing body.

And Congress—as a result of experience in the early days of the Republic—set up a system of seniority in both houses so that the oldest members, in length of service, become the chairmen of committees. One of the drawbacks of the system of seniority is that in some parts of the country a minority group controls the elections of congressmen and senators. I am certain the time is coming when all congressmen and senators will be elected by a majority of constituents enjoying full civil rights.

The First Congress of the United States sought to set up rules by which chairmen of committees were to be chosen by a majority vote of the full membership of the Senate and the House, respectively. This caused so much confusion, as a result of personal bickering, that Congress could not get down to business. After this experience, it was decided by the Second Congress that seniority was the more practical approach.

Time and again in the history of the country, a few members of Congress have thwarted the will of the people. Eventually those who thwart the will of the people are eliminated. I can remember back in the 1890's when all the old economic royalists were in control of the Senate. It was a rich man's club. It is no longer that. We have changed the manner of selecting senators. Now, senators are elected directly by the people, but continuity remains under the system of staggering the election of senators every two years. And one of the great advantages of continuity through seniority is that the ablest and best informed members are available to help initiate new members into the going business of the legislature without loss of time.

Every now and then, men in that body rise to such

great heights of influence and service that they become national institutions in their own right. Such a man is Sam Rayburn of Texas, who has been Speaker of the House of Representatives longer than any man in history, with a brilliant record of liberal legislative authorship to his credit.

The most permanent and visible link of the continuity of our system of government is, of course, our Civil Service, which establishes a corps of officials and workers, not subject to dismissal for political reasons, and on whom the elected representatives of the people can depend for the continued maintenance of government operations.

8

What to Do
with Former Presidents

ONE of the first things I thought about after returning to
my home in Independence was how the unique experience and special knowledge that a former President ac-
quires could be put to some use to serve the country.

Long before I became President, I had thought very
much about this. While in the Senate, I explored with a
number of my colleagues a proposal to allow former Presidents to appear on the floor of the Senate and address that
body whenever they thought they had something to say.
But nothing came of it.

Within the first few weeks of my succession to the Presidency, I saw an opportunity to put to use the special
experiences of a former President. In the closing stages of
the war in Europe, we faced the responsibility of feeding
millions of victims of that war. I naturally turned to Herbert
Hoover, who had demonstrated in the First World War that
he had the skill and the humanity to save millions of people

117

threatened with starvation. The services of former President Hoover in this instance were timely and important, and there was no starvation in many countries as a result of his efforts.

I shall never be able to understand the long neglect of Herbert Hoover, no matter what the events and circumstances of his Administration were. How history may eventually assess his Administration we ought to leave to history.

Politically and economically, Hoover and I are on opposite sides on basic issues. But I hold him in high esteem as a man of character and capacity and talent, and he deserved better treatment at the hands of his own party. I thought, too, that President Roosevelt might have invited him to join the bipartisan group that Roosevelt so wisely set up to administer the war effort.

Like all men who occupied the office of President, Mr. Hoover was just like the rest of us. He wanted to do exactly what was right. I might say that I think one of his difficulties was that in a political way he started at the top instead of at the bottom. It would be just like my starting an engineering career without knowing anything about engineering.

A man has to know politics the same as he does any other business, and I think the principal cause of Mr. Hoover's troubles and the cause of the troubles of a great many men who started at the top, including Henry Wallace, was that they did not know the political set-up from the ground up.

Early in 1945, when I had succeeded to the Presidency in the midst of the world's most terrible war, the food situation in Europe became alarming. I knew what I had to do and I knew just the man I wanted to help me. I had read in the Washington newspapers a small item saying that former President Hoover was in town and staying at the Shoreham Hotel.

I immediately picked up the telephone on the desk of the Oval Room at the White House and asked the chief operator, Mrs. Hackmeister, to connect me with the hotel. Hackie, as she is called, was a little taken aback. She asked whom I wanted to reach, since it was customary for the White House switchboard to get through to the person the President wanted to talk to before putting the President on.

I asked Hackie just to put me through to the Shoreham. After I got the Shoreham Hotel switchboard, I asked to be connected with Mr. Hoover. When a voice answered, I said: "How are you, Mr. President?"

There was a pause and then the voice said, "Who is this?"

"This is Harry Truman," I answered. Again there was a pause.

Finally, Mr. Hoover said: "Oh, Mr. *President*. How are you?"

"I heard you were in town, Mr. President," I said, "and I called to ask if you would care to come over and see your old home."

There was another pause. Then Mr. Hoover said: "I would not impose on your time in days like these, but I do appreciate your kindness in telephoning me and inviting me over."

I quickly replied: "I'd be glad to come over to see you."

At this, Mr. Hoover said: "I cannot let you do that, but I would be glad to come over if you will fix the time."

"Well," I answered, "I took the liberty of anticipating

you. I already have a car on the way over to your hotel to bring you to the White House."

WITHIN the time that it took for the car to bring Mr. Hoover to the White House, I arranged to have him received by the staff at the entrance of the executive wing where my office was located. But Mr. Hoover had arrived at the main entrance of the White House, where he was recognized only by the chief usher. Someone asked, "Who was that tall man rushing through the corridor to the executive office?"

"That was President Hoover," the chief usher said, "and he didn't need anyone to show him how to get to the Oval Room." Mr. Hoover had gone down the corridor and up the stairs to where we were waiting for him.

We had a very cordial meeting, and then I told him I had something that I wanted to discuss with him which I thought was for the welfare of the world. I told him about the reports of starvation in Europe and the crop failures in South Africa, South America, Indonesia and other rice-raising countries. I asked him if he would not try to help organize an effort to get food to all the needy, for we could not allow anyone anywhere to starve if we could possibly avoid it.

Mr. Hoover immediately volunteered to help me do something about it. He said that he would return the following day with Dr. Julius Klein, who had been his assistant at the White House, to plan whatever was needed.

As he left, I told the former President that I would be glad to have him stay at the White House if he would care to, but he declined, saying that he would rather stay at the hotel. This is the same answer I would have given if I had been in his place. The former President was always welcome to come to the White House, and I saw to it that every time he came to Washington he was extended every courtesy and that a White House car would always be at his disposal.

Herbert Hoover did a magnificent job for this country, and for other nations, in helping to prevent the starvation of millions of people. And when this work was launched and eventually taken over by the relevant government agencies, Mr. Hoover expressed a readiness to assume any other tasks I thought he could perform for the government of the United States.

I did want him later for another very important task, and that was to help streamline the executive departments and the new agencies that had been created to meet the various war needs. The government of the United States had grown so rapidly during the war that duplication and waste were inevitable and needed correction. Such a streamlining would require, of course, new statutes and Congressional action.

This streamlining operation, now known as the Hoover Commission, made a great contribution then, as well as in the following years, to the operation and organization of the government. Only a man of Hoover's talents, with the very important experience he had as President, could have achieved so difficult a task with such marked results.

President Hoover's contributions again impressed me with the fact that a man who has had the experience of a President, or a Vice President, or a Speaker of the House, gets a chance to become much more familiar with our government than any one else. These are the men to whom we must look for help and counsel. That is why we must not shelve or thrust into obscurity men with such unique experience. And least of all, our former Presidents.

FOR a long time, I had in the back of my mind something much broader in concept about what contributions former Presidents could make to the nation beyond the occasional services such as Mr. Hoover rendered. I was not thinking in terms of what the nation could do for outgoing Presidents. They have already enjoyed honors greater than they could expect. What I was thinking about was what further benefits the nation and the people might get from these men who have acquired an enormous amount of knowledge and insight into the operations and aims of government. Certainly we ought not waste all these assets. Personally, I feel that, as a former President, I would wish to acknowledge my debt and gratitude for the great honor the people bestowed on me by rendering any further service I could.

When I was President, I often wondered whether it would not be a good idea for former Presidents to be designated senators-at-large to sit in the Senate and take part in debate but with no right to vote. In this way, the Senate would have the benefit of their judgment and views without upsetting the voting balance of the states.

I should not have been taken by surprise when some of my friends who knew my views on this subject suggested that, upon the expiration of my term, I might consider running for a regular Senate seat from Missouri; this was my old seat and was up in 1952.

That was certainly not the idea I had in mind, although my friends may have been thinking of John Quincy Adams, the sixth President, who ran for Congress in 1831 after retiring as President. Adams served as a congressman from Massachusetts from 1831 to 1848.

Even if the idea of running for the Senate had appealed to me, I would not have considered it because, when I was due to leave the White House, Missouri had two able and distinguished senators in Thomas C. Hennings, Jr. and Stuart Symington.

But I kept turning over in my mind, after returning to private life, what might be the best way for the nation to make use of former Presidents. I realized that there were many difficulties which were rooted in tradition and politics, not to mention the reluctance of certain of our Presidents to counsel with their predecessors.

I THINK there is one way to overcome these obstacles so that we can stop the waste of a vast storehouse of experience. This would also help bridge a certain gap in the continuity of our government. And this should no longer be a personal matter to be decided upon by the whim of whoever happens to be the President.

I would therefore make the following suggestion:

Congress should pass enabling legislation designating former Presidents of the United States *as Free Members of the Congress.*

These Free Members would have the right to sit on the
floor of the Senate and of the House on all occasions.

They would have the right to take part in debate, subject, of course, to the parliamentary procedures in each house.

The Free Members *would not have the right to vote.*

They *would* have the right to sit in on any meetings of
any committee, subcommittee or joint committee of both
houses and take part in discussions. Here, too, they would
not have the right of vote.

Free Members would be assigned suitable office space
in the congressional buildings.

I THINK, too, that we should consider some provision for
making use of former Vice Presidents and retired Speakers of
the House. In the early years of the Republic, Vice Presidents
often became Presidents, having been marked especially to
succeed to that office. Since the days of the Civil War, Vice
Presidents have not played the same role, although as Vice
President Thomas Marshall put it, there was only a heartbeat between him and the Presidency, and several Vice
Presidents, including myself, did become Presidents—seven
in all—by succession on the death of the President.

In the world today, and in view of our nation's position
in it, the Vice President must be, and is, better prepared and
more fully informed than were many of the Vice Presidents
of the past. In the event that they do not become Presidents,
we ought to make full use of their experience and talent.

I have heard it suggested that former Presidents be used
on diplomatic missions either as ambassadors or members of

delegations to international conferences. But this would be a mistake. No former President ought to undertake such a role. Foreign policy is the responsibility solely of the President of the United States and he should not be interfered with. And a former President would be inclined to interfere and express opinions because he had once been making foreign policy on his own and might find himself not in full agreement with the instructions of the incumbent President. A former President should therefore not be put in a position to interfere in foreign policy but only to give his opinions and judgments based on his experience. The floor of the Congress would, of course, be the best place for that purpose.

Since I left the White House, I have been invited to appear before several congressional committees. I testified before the Senate Committee on Foreign Relations on the tenth anniversary of the United Nations and was pleased to express my opinion of what could be done to strengthen that international body. I also appeared before a House committee considering the repeal of the constitutional amendment limiting a President to two terms.

I appeared before a House committee to support my proposal contained in a bill to provide for the indexing and microfilming of all Presidential papers now and in the future. Parts of sixteen sets of Presidential papers are in the Library of Congress. A start has been made on indexing and microfilming them. Several committees have called on me at Kansas City to get my testimony on certain bills. And I was always glad to appear before them at their convenience.

This experience with congressional committees again proved to me how much more sense it would make for a former President to be available to the Congress in Washington on a regular basis. The former President, of course, could not be expected to sit still, just waiting to be called on for an expression of opinion. More often he would want to speak up on matters which he might deem necessary to bring to the attention of the Congress.

Arguments and debate are what make a free government, and a former President could be counted on to stimulate and even provoke debate. Where there is no debate there is dictatorship. Of course, I would not propose that a former President, if he were a Free Member of Congress having no right to vote, be entitled to filibuster.

Looking back over the history of our country, I have noted that too many of our Presidents were bitterly assailed while in office and some were not spared from scorn even after retirement. This is one of the harsh sides of American political life and our partisan aproach to free government. Partisan as I am, I deplore this.

I believe my proposal would not only utilize men of talent and experience who could render valued public service but would also cushion the shock when an abrupt change in administration takes place.

9

My Views on Religion

I HAVE been a voluntary member of the Baptist Church since I was eighteen years old.

When I came home in 1953, I helped to rebuild the new Baptist Church in Grandview, to which my family had always belonged. But I have found that I cannot appear regularly in church, either in Grandview or Independence, without feeling like a showpiece or someone on exhibit. So I do not go as often as I would want to.

People ought to go to church to worship God—not to see some mortal who is there.

From time to time, I yield to an invitation to preach from a church pulpit. I did this not long ago when, in response to an invitation from a Methodist congregation in Dallas, Texas, I told the congregation my thoughts about religion and a moral code.

My mother and father were Baptists, so was my Grandfather Truman and my Grandmother Young. Grandma Truman died many years before I was born. She was also a Baptist.

My Grandfather Young belonged to no church, but he supported many of them—Baptist, Methodist, Campbellite and Presbyterian. They all met in the old church out in front of the house on the family farm on Sunday. Grandfather Young told me when I was six that all of them wanted to arrive at the same place but they had to fight about it to see who had the inside track with the Almighty. His opinion was that none of them had any special "in" with God Almighty because He would make His own decision about who had been good or bad on this planet.

My Grandfather Truman felt the same way—but thought that the Baptists had the best chance to arrive at happiness beyond the grave. Both Grandfather Truman and Grandfather Young were good men, as good as they come. They had firm opinions about right and wrong, and they practiced what they preached and believed.

All my family disliked a hypocrite. My Grandfather Young once told me, "When a man spends Saturday night and Sunday doing too much howling and praying, you had better go home and lock your smoke house."

Both of these men were trustful souls and never failed to help anyone around them who needed help. My father and mother were the same way. I never saw them turn a tramp away hungry, and we had many applications for food at the back door at the time I was growing up.

My mother took my brother and sister and me to Sunday school as soon as it was possible after we settled in Independence in 1890. It happened that the First Presbyterian Church was closest to our home. So we went there to Sunday school. That is where I met the beautiful blue-eyed golden-haired young lady, Virginia Elizabeth Wallace, who

spent the rest of her life with me. She was five and I was six.
I sat in front of her, and now and then she used to tap me
over the head with a ruler.

I think a further example of how highly individualistic
my people were, and how self-reliant and independent they
were in their personal views, is illustrated by a story told me
by my uncle when I was eighteen.

I was named for my uncle, my mother's brother, whose
name was Harrison Young. I was given the diminutive form
of Harry and, so that I could have two initials in my given
name, the letter "S" was added. I was very fond of my Uncle
Harrison. He was a big man, a little over six feet in height,
and he weighed 201 pounds. He was as strong as a wrestler
and he was a very good story teller. He did not attend church
regularly.

I once told my uncle that I was going to the field to get
an armful of green corn so that we could have corn pudding.
He asked me if I knew the record number of ears of corn a
man had ever eaten at one sitting.

I told him I did not know. Then he told me a story about
a pal of his who had the record on a bet by eating thirteen
roasting ears. This fellow contracted a severe stomach-ache
and had to send for the doctor. The doctor worked over him
the rest of the night, and in the morning told him that he
had better send for the preacher and do a little praying. The
man was in such pain that he sent for the parson. The parson
prayed for him, and recommended that he also pray for
himself.

But the stricken man told the preacher he was not a
praying man and did not think he could do it. However, as
the excruciating pain persisted, the man decided to make an

attempt. He got down on his knees in the old-fashioned revival manner, and this was his petition to the Almighty: "Oh, Lord, I am in great pain and misery. I have eaten thirteen roasting ears of corn and I don't seem to be able to take care of them. I am praying to you for help. And Lord, I am not like those howling church members in the Amen corner. If you will just relieve me of seven of these ears of corn, I'll try to handle the other six by myself."

WHEN I became President of the United States, my church affiliation became a subject of national interest. That was understandable. I was familiar with the church-going of former Presidents, and knew where and when they worshipped. When I first went to Washington, I attended the First Baptist Church on Sixteenth Street whenever I was in town, and always sat in the back rows. But when I moved to 1600 Pennsylvania Avenue, I found that everything I did or did not do was subject for news and comment.

When I returned as President for the first time to the First Baptist Church, I was shocked by the appearance of newsmen and photographers assigned to cover me; along with them came many curiosity-seekers who obviously had not come to worship. I tried to be as inconspicuous as I could, for I did not wish to intrude on the services. I instructed the Secret Service men to keep the photographers from following me into church, and I sat where I hoped attention would not be diverted from the services.

But when that failed, I stopped going to the First Baptist Church and attended services when I could at the chapels of Walter Reed Hospital or Bethesda, where photographers were barred. It was difficult to have privacy in church while I was President, and I guess I should not have expected to avoid curiosity in church when I came home.

I HAVE had to meet and deal with many people and events, all of which has given me an opportunity to take a long look at life. Young students who come to see me at the Library in Independence often ask me whether we have changed much morally and spiritually since the beginnings of civilization.

I tell them that, as I see it, the human animal has not changed very much. He has to be guided in the proper direction under a moral code, and then there must be some machinery to make him live within that moral code. A man cannot have character unless he lives within a fundamental system of morals that creates character.

There are many moral and religious codes in the world. In my opinion, the moral code of the Christian religion is about as good as there is. The Mohammedans have a code based closely on the Christian precepts, and the Buddhists have a moral code that is excellent, as do the Confucians.

I have been asked whether the failure of Christianity is not partly responsible for the growing spread of Communism in the world. I cannot agree that Christianity has been a failure. But ruthless men have been able to impose Communism on helpless people because of the absence of Christianity and the lack of a code that upholds the freedom and dignity of the individual. No nation has ever adopted Communism by the choice of its people in a free election.

This is not to say that Christianity has not had its difficulties throughout its history, but there are always difficulties in everything that pertains to man. There has been terrible bloodshed over Christianity, brought about by struggles between sects and denominations. Those who resorted to wars to inflict their kind of Christianity upon other faiths or denominations did not really understand Christianity.

We have gone a long way toward civilization and religious tolerance, and we have a good example in this country. Here the many Protestant denominations, the Catholic Church and the Greek Orthodox Church do not seek to destroy one another in physical violence just because they do not interpret every verse of the Bible in exactly the same way. Here we now have the freedom of all religions, and I hope that never again will we have a repetition of religious bigotry, as we have had in certain periods of our own history. There is no room for that kind of foolishness here. Under our Republic there is separation of church and state, guaranteed under the Constitution by the First Amendment.

WHILE there are disturbing things taking place in many parts of the world, I continue to be optimistic about the future. It is only fair to say that I am an optimist by disposition, but my confidence in the future is based more on my reading of history and the evolution of man's works. I have never seen pessimists make anything work, or contribute anything of lasting value. It takes idealists to make the world work, because eventually some of the ideas they develop are put into practice to help mankind.

One idea that has always seemed to me worth trying is to bring about the active cooperation of the leaders and the followers of the great religious faiths of the world. If such a common religious and moral front would be organized, a vital force for the advancement of peace could be harnessed.

Minor, and even major, differences in how we choose to worship God strike me as being of relatively little importance in the face of an aggressive foe threatening to destroy all freedom of worship and other individual liberties.

In 1948, when I was President, I tried to interest the religious leaders of the world in such a move. I sent Myron G. Taylor, whom I had previously reappointed as the President's personal representative to the Vatican, on a special mission to Pope Pius XII to outline my thoughts on this subject. I had some private exchanges of views with Protestant prelates, among them Bishop G. Bromley Oxnam and Dr. Samuel McCrea Cavert. I spoke with several prominent Jewish leaders, and contact had been made with spiritual authorities in the Moslem world. I sought to establish communications with leaders of other faiths, including the Dalai Lama of Tibet.

The proposal made a deep impression in most quarters, but there was some hesitation by a few leaders of groups here and abroad. I realized that more time would be needed to convince these leaders of the desirability of a common religious and moral front. But it was not possible for me to pursue it further during the remainder of my term of office.

I feel that an important opportunity was missed, and that those who had misgivings about such a religious and moral alliance ought to realize that a foe common to them all was trying to destroy them all. I still hope to see the religious leaders themselves initiate a move to bring about close co-ordination to serve the needs of peace and humankind against an unparalleled threat to all religion.

SINCE I have been home, I have received requests from different religious groups to meet with them and sometimes to join with them in their services. I have accepted as many of these invitations as I have been able to work into my schedule. Their number was so large as to surprise me, and the invitations came from many different denominations and faiths.

I began one week, for example, by talking to twelve hundred students at a small Baptist College. The following day I addressed sixty-five hundred young people in the presence of Cardinal Cushing, Archbishop of Boston, at a convention of the Catholic Youth in Kansas City. The next day I went to Columbia, Missouri, to dedicate a plaque at the Jewish Chapel at the University of Missouri in honor of Eddie Jacobson, my long-time friend and my one time part-ner in business.

I then flew to Dallas, Texas, twenty-four hours later, and was the lay speaker at the Elmwood Methodist Church there. I preached to the congregation on the moral code from the twentieth chapter of Exodus, the fifth chapter of Deuter-onomy, Isaiah II, Joel III and the Sermon on the Mount.

This, in part, is what I said from the pulpit:

"I came here this morning at the request of your pastor

and your bishop to discuss with you some of the things in which I am vitally interested, particularly the method by which our government functions, because every function of the government is tied in to the spirit of the Bible.

"My mother, married in 1881 to my father, had a great big gold-back Bible with the first part of the Revised Version. One column represented the Bible as it should be, the other side was the Revised Version. And I got a chance to read them both.

"If I wanted to find out anything in either Testament, I didn't read the Revised Version, I read the translation that was made under King James of Great Britain. That was the greatest thing he ever did in his life, and the reason for that, in my opinion, is the fact that that, along with Shakespeare, established the English language as we know it.

"It is one of the most beautifully translated versions of the Bible that there is. I was presented with a Vulgate and a copy of the Gutenberg Bible, and I was sworn in on that Latin Book. And as you know, I had them turn to the twentieth chapter of Exodus.

"I was talking to someone the other day, believe it or not an educated young man, and I told him he had better read the twentieth chapter of Exodus, it would do him good. And he said, 'What is Exodus?' What are you going to do? I think every youngster ought to be told by his mother and father to read at least one book until he gets all the way over to Revelations. It won't do him any harm.

"The fundamental basis of all government is in this Book right here, and it started with Moses on the Mount. He was familiar with the government of his day—that is, the Babylonian Law-giver, Hammurabi, who lived five or six thousand years ago, and established the first code for government. And Moses was educated in Egypt, where they had one of the greatest governments of ancient history. But he never forgot the God-given law which is in this Book, and he taught it all the time.

"You know everybody is terribly ungrateful, and they forget, and they forget, and they forget. That is the reason these things have to be continually repeated, and I was particularly intrigued with the laws that are set out in the Old and the New Testaments.

"You take that twentieth chapter of Exodus, and the sixth chapter of Deuteronomy, and the prophets, Isaiah, and Micah, and Joel; then turn over to the Sermon on the Mount. The man that was preaching that Sermon on the Mount was reiterating what the law and the prophets set forth.

"I wish my mother could have been here today to hear a Southern Methodist church sing 'The Battle Hymn of the Republic.' That shows we are really together again. That was one of the war songs that was sung in the War Between the States. She never called it the Civil War; she called it the War Between the States, and she died unreconstructed.

"She wouldn't give me, or my father either, permission to join the National Guard because she was afraid I would have to wear a blue uniform. And I did have to wear a blue uniform, and I went out to see my grandmother one day. She said, 'Harry, that's the first time since those Kansas Redlegs burned my house that a uniform of that color has been in this house and don't you bring it back.' And I didn't either.

"I want to read you a couple of extracts from the old prophets—one from the great prophets, one from the minor prophets. Do you know why they are called great and minor prophets? The great prophets, oh, they had fifteen, twenty or thirty pages in the Old Book, and the minor prophets only had three or four pages. But the minor prophets were just as great. They were all trying to get the people to understand that they were on this earth for a purpose, and that in order to accomplish that purpose they must follow a code of morals.

"Do you remember, in John Bunyan's *Pilgrim's Progress*, there was a certain fellow who was always looking down, hoping he would find a treasure, and all he had to do was look up and he would find it there? That's the difference between a people with a moral code and a people without one.

"Now here is one of the things that is always being quoted. You will find it in Isaiah 2:4; listen to what it says: 'He shall judge among the nations, and shall rebuke many people; and they shall beat their swords into plowshares, and their spears into pruning hooks; nation shall not lift up sword against nation, neither shall they learn war any more.'

"Let me read something to you from another prophet. He is one of the minor prophets, one of the great ones. Listen to what he says, this will interest you very, very much: 'Beat your plowshares into swords and your pruning hooks into spears. Let the weak say, I am strong.' Which one do you want? It depends on what the condition is. This last part was read to you from Joel; you will find it in 3:10. He was trying to get the people to understand that they had to protect their government if they expected ever to have a free government.

"That is all we have ever done in this country. We have never, never in our history tried to make people come under a rule who didn't want to stay under that rule. Texas is a shining example. Voluntarily, they became a part of the United States of America. The greatest man in the history of Texas, from the beginning, was an old fellow by the name of Sam Houston. He believed in the government of the United States.

"I know some things about your history, the same as you know something about Missouri's history. Now, I want to say to you, Missouri has been very good to Texas. Missouri has furnished you with a lot of things including the blue-bonnets, and they sowed them all, if you know what I mean. Missouri, you know, has made one of the greatest contributions west of the Mississippi that any state could possibly make. I don't know whether you know it or not, but nearly every state that was created out of the Louisiana Purchase, was induced to adopt the Missouri code of laws. Do you know where that code came from? It came from William Penn's state, Pennsylvania. Ben Franklin helped to write that code.

"The most interesting thing to me is over here in the fifth, sixth and seventh chapters of the Gospel according to St. Matthew. Here are some of the things that impressed me. I am going to read the whole thing again—then, read it again —then, read it again. It won't harm you to read it a hundred times, because the more you read it, the more of it will stick in your head.

"It says, 'Blessed are the meek for they shall inherit the earth. . . . Blessed are the meek for they shall inherit the earth.' I have yet to see a meek politician, but that is what it says here. 'Blessed are the merciful, for they shall obtain mercy.' Right here and now, what's greater than that? And it says, 'Blessed are the peacemakers, for they shall be called the children of God.' That is what we all want to be. That is exactly what we all want to be. We want to be peacemakers. Not just individually, but internationally.

"Do you know what? Do you know where the Good Neighbor Policy of the United States originated? It originated in the tenth chapter of St. Luke.

"If you will read this tenth chapter of Luke, you will find out exactly what a good neighbor means. It means to treat your neighbor as you yourself would like to be treated. Makes no difference whether he is of another race or another creed or another color. He is still your neighbor. Luke gives us the best definition of it, and you don't have to go anywhere else to find it.

"I go around preaching that politically and every other way. I am here this morning to try to get you to understand that I believe what these things say and I try to act like it. I don't know whether I have or not. You will find plenty of people who say I haven't done a thing right. That is none of their problem. That is mine. I have to make my peace with the Lord myself, nobody else can do it for me."

WHEN, on my return, our former cook Vietta Garr came to see me about talking before the National Negro Baptist Convention in Independence, I said I would be especially pleased to appear with them.

This is, in part, what I said at that Baptist meeting:

"I am a Baptist by education and by the belief that John the Baptist recognized and baptized the Savior of the world,

Jesus. And, my friends, he did not sprinkle him with Jordan water; he reverently lowered him bodily below the surface of the sacred Jordan and raised him as a symbol that sin could be washed away.

"The Jews had long been awaiting a prophet who would give them a revival of the teachings of Moses, Samuel, Amos and Isaiah, and when He came, they failed to recognize Him. He came to rescue the poor and the indigent from the special-privilege classes. He was born in a manger. He grew up as the son of a carpenter and was one Himself. But remember, He carried His mission to the people who needed the mercy of God.

"He constantly called attention to the Law and the prophets. He told the people, who believed that they were better than the poor, where they stood. He called attention to the widow's mite as much more welcome to God the Father than was the gold contribution of the Pharisees. He also said to go into your closet and pray, and God will hear you. He called attention to those who made a great display of their religion and called them hypocrites.

"He reminded them of the Good Samaritan who had helped his neighbor—and Samaritans were, in that day in Jerusalem, regarded as people of your color have been in some parts of the United States. You should be proud of your color. If I were black or red or yellow, I would do everything I could to make people understand that what is in the heart and the mind is what counts with Almighty God—not the color of the skin.

"Jesus Christ preached the Law and the prophets—the twentieth chapter of Exodus, the fifth chapter of Deuteronomy, the preachings of Amos, Micah, Isaiah and Jeremiah.

Study the Sermon on the Mount, the fifth, sixth and seventh chapters of the Gospel according to St. Matthew, the tenth chapter of St. Luke, and then turn back to Matthew 22:15 and find obedience to the law of the land.

"The Old Testament and the New will give you a way of life that will cause you to live happily."

10

H.S.T.: Roving Teacher (First Seminar)

Almost as soon as I settled down at home, I found myself drawn into the unexpected role of a roving teacher. Actually, I had hoped that after I left the White House I would, in some way, find an opportunity to talk to young people about the operation of our government and the function and meaning of the Presidency.

But I had not anticipated that this desire on my part would develop into anything that would be formal, scholarly or professorial. Even when I received several invitations to head colleges or universities, I could not entertain them seriously, because I did not have the formal education I felt one needed for such a post.

I took the same attitude when I was asked to undertake a college or university professorship. Besides, there were many other things I wanted to do. What I did want to do more than anything else was to put in as much time as I could with youngsters, primarily in group meetings where we would have an opportunity to discuss freely the questions they had in mind about our form of government in these days of great historic changes.

Invitations to lecture began to reach me from every part of the country upon my return to Independence. They came from the oldest schools of the East, as well as universities of all sections of the country, and they came from the middle-sized and small land grant colleges, in which I was especially interested.

My only regret is that I have been unable to accept all of these invitations. Of those that I did accept, I have tried to select representative schools of every geographic part of the country. In this way I have found myself becoming a kind of roving teacher. This is a role that has given me a great deal of happiness and satisfaction.

To me, there is nothing more rewarding than to stand before young people and find them so vitally interested in everything pertaining to the affairs of the country and the world. I do not share the concern of some critics that our young people lack the quality and the character of former generations. If these critics could share with me the excitement and stimulus that I get from the intelligent and provocative questions these youngsters put to me, they would not be so preoccupied with the so-called "beat" or "lost" generation.

What impresses me more than anything else in the questions they ask me is the range and variety of the interests of the young people. I find myself, on each occasion after a talk with students, as invigorated and as alert as I used to feel after a White House press conference. I learn as much from the questions of the students as to what is really going on in their minds and in their community as I did from the questions White House correspondents would put to me about what they thought was going on in the country and what the public was thinking about.

I have picked out a number of questions and answers at random which I think throw a fair light on the range of interests of the young people in our colleges and universities. I wish there were space to include all of the questions and answers I have recorded.

The selections which follow constitute the first publication of my "Classroom Seminars." These took place in many of the sessions around the country and in the Truman Library auditorium. The answers to the questions do not, of course, represent a comprehensive treatment of the subject raised. And they are set down here in the quick and spontaneous give-and-take manner that characterized these "seminars" between the students and this roving teacher.

These are some of the questions they asked:

Q. Here, in a world divided and in turmoil, isn't the leadership pretty well limited to a few elder statesmen? Where are the new leaders to come from?

A. The new leaders will come to the top when the times call for them. This has always happened throughout history. New leaders always come to the top when they are required. The main difficulty with the oldsters is that they never know when to give up. The best time for a man to step out of a position is when he has accomplished what he thinks is his program. The main trouble with most of these people is they want to maintain control after they're past the time when they *can* maintain control.

Q. But isn't the history of the world full of important work done by oldsters who have had experience? Aren't there oldsters who are mentally alert and in their prime even if they are not at their prime physically?

A. These experienced oldsters you are talking about who are mentally efficient should not be ignored. They should be listened to by the rising leaders planning their own program. The rising leaders can then make up their own minds, which is what they always do anyway. The youngsters never learn anything except by experience.

Q. Hasn't the office of the Vice President of the United States become more important in recent times and weren't you the first President to ask the Vice President to sit in at all Cabinet meetings?

A. In the early days of the Republic, the Vice President was usually groomed to succeed to the Presidency. John Adams was Vice President under Washington, and Jefferson was Vice President under John Adams. In the years after that, the Vice President was not given much opportunity to take active part in the administration. It was President Roosevelt and not I who initiated the practice of having the Vice President take part in Cabinet meetings. Roosevelt not only assigned special duties to Vice President Wallace, making him head of the Board of Economic Warfare, but invited him to Cabinet meetings. When I became Vice President, I was invited to sit in with the Cabinet every time it met, but as you know, that was for a short period of time. And then I continued this same arrangement with Vice President Barkley, always remembering that Thomas R. Marshall cautioned us that a Vice President is only one heartbeat from the White House.

Q. What sort of a man should we look for when we are searching for a Presidential candidate?

A. Well, the first thing you've got to be sure of is that you have a man who is honorable and who has broad experience in government. Any man who aspires to public office ought to have a background of political effort in order to get that office. To secure that political background, he must have worked in the precincts in the county and in the state in which he lived. And in politics you must choose people who have had experience if you expect to have an administrator who knows what to do and how to do it. But you can't tell what's inside of a man until you put him into office. If you take a man from a minor position and put him into a job of responsibility, sometimes he will turn out to be a success and sometimes he'll turn out to be an utter fool. There is no way you can tell how the mind of a man is going to work. You have to take a chance on a person, whether you appoint or elect him to high position. Experience shows many make good and a great many don't. That's the difficulty. It's the human animal all over again, and you do the best you can in trying to find the right man.

Q. Isn't there some way to put Presidential candidates through some preliminary test?

A. I don't know of any preliminary test that would tell us anything for sure. Now in the old days, succession was based on birth and position. Some of our Presidents who got there on this basis turned out to be wonderful men and great leaders. One thing I am certain about, there's nothing in our history, so far as I am able to find out, that shows that a man can be trained to be President of the United States, or that we could ensure that he would ever become President even if trained for the job, because there are so many factors that enter into the making of a President. And I'd like to add that, on the whole, we have had an unusually high percentage of greatness in the thirty-three men who have been President.

Q. Do you think adequate justice has been done to the lives of all the Presidents in the books that have been written about them?

A. No, I do not. I think a striking case in point is the life of Andrew Johnson. Had it not been for Stryker's research and work on the life of Johnson, people would have had the wrong impression of him as President. Johnson was one of the great Presidents, and he was in a terrifically bad position. He was elected on the American Union ticket with Lincoln. He was a Democrat and Lincoln was a Whig, a Republican of that day. When Johnson became President on Lincoln's assassination, there was a band of radicals in the Congress, headed by old Thad Stevens, whose objective was to persecute the states that had tried to leave the Union. Andrew

Johnson, on the other hand, wanted to carry out the policies of Abraham Lincoln. Johnson was a Constitution-minded President and he knew more about the Constitution of the United States, I think, than any other President up to his time.

Q. Who in your opinion was the most abused President?

A. You may be surprised, but it was the father of our country, George Washington. He was roundly abused for everything he did when he was trying to unify the Colonies into a national government. Some of the Colonies wanted to maintain their individual rights and independence. Washington sought to make a nation out of them, and he did. He was subjected to so much abuse that he insisted on quitting at the end of his second term. He could have had a third term or a fourth, had he wanted them. As a matter of fact, he wanted to quit after his first Administration, but he was persuaded to stay on for another round.

Q. Why do people in political audiences always call to you, "Give 'em Hell Harry"?

A. Well, that started out in the Northwest, in Seattle, Washington. It was in 1948, and we were holding an enthusiastic meeting there when some man with a great big voice cried from the galleries, "Give 'em hell, Harry!" I told him at that time, and I have been repeating it ever since, that I have never deliberately given anybody hell. I just tell the truth on the opposition—and they think it's hell.

Q. Would you say then that this is an apt description of your style of political campaigning, which has also sometimes been called a slashing attack?

A. I can't go along with that description. It is an attack, of course, but it is not an attack on individuals. It's an attack based on principles. I never said anything against my opponents personally. But I attacked the things they stood for, if I didn't approve of them, and their actions as public servants. I never attacked them as individuals.

Q. Do you think our national Presidential conventions are conducted in the way they ought to be?

A. Well, that's American democracy at its highest pitch. You take these conventions apart and study them, and you'll find they are the most interesting development in the history of the country. National conventions started 'way back in Jackson's Administration, when he insisted on a Democratic convention being held instead of allowing the Congressional caucus to nominate a man for President, as had been done up to then. This was when he was having difficulty with John Quincy Adams and Henry Clay in 1824. The convention method of nominating a President—with certain changes in the rules—has continued since that time. It has proven one of the most effective ways for the people to find out exactly what politicians stand for.

Q. Does a national convention provide machinery to express the real choice of the political party? How do you

avoid confusion where so many favorite sons are presented as candidates?

A. I have always favored open conventions, where every duly qualified favorite son or candidate has the right to be presented to the convention. And when he is so presented, he has to get up and show what he has and what he stands for. If he doesn't show it, he's out.

Q. **Then do you think that having state primaries, where the favorite son is always in a position to crowd out somebody who is more of a national figure, is a good thing?**

A. No. I'll tell you what the trouble is with state primaries. They nominate their favorite son, and the delegates who are elected for the national convention are tied to that candidate. They have no right to change and vote for the man they might prefer in some instances. Every state convention nominates someone for President or agrees to support someone for President. Some of the states even invoke a unit rule which compels minority delegates to be for the person nominated by the state convention. And that has the same effect as the primary. I do not believe in the unit rule, and I don't approve of Presidential primaries for the simple reason that these state conventions and state primaries bind delegations to one candidate. In effect, they go back to the old legislative caucus which Jackson ruled out. The objective of a national convention is to give all the delegates an unrestricted chance to express their opinions of their final choices. When they cannot do that, then it can only lead to split and deadlocked conventions, often preventing the best choice.

Q. Are the delegates that come to the national convention truly representative of the party?

A. I don't think there's much question about that. If the Democratic party isn't properly represented in these conventions, and *I* think it is, it's because the people are too lazy to go to the various precinct, county and state meetings to see that the proper representatives of the people are selected. I don't have any sympathy with anyone who complains about what's done when he never takes any interest in it.

Q. Doesn't it take large sums of money to nominate and elect a man to office, and doesn't that pose a serious problem to a candidate without funds?

A. Having a certain amount of money for expenses is necessary, but I don't think money is the deciding element in a campaign. I never had enough money to run a campaign in my county where I first held public office. I never had enough money to run a campaign for the Senate. And I never had enough money to run a campaign for the Presidency in 1948. Yet we won.

Q. What does it take mostly to win an election?

A. Well, it takes a candidate who understands what the people want. That's worth more than all the money he may be able to put together.

Q. How does a candidate get his story over to the people without the use of a lot of money?

A. He just goes out and talks to the people. Sometimes he has to go into debt rather than obligate his friends. It took me about ten years in the Senate to pay off the debts I had incurred in the campaign. I had expenses connected with travel, telephone, postage and printing. I had contributions, of course, as every man who runs for office must have. But all my contributions were small and inadequate.

Q. You say that to win, a candidate must understand what the people want. Just what do you mean by what the people want? Are you suggesting that the candidate should cater to everything the voters want?

A. Certainly not. What I mean is that a candidate must have a program and must make that program perfectly plain so that everybody understands it. He must try to persuade people to his program. If the majority of the people agree, then he is bound to win because he will be expressing what the people want. But, of course, he cannot please everybody. If he tries to please everybody, he will please nobody. What the people want is leadership, and they expect fair treatment in carrying out their needs. They want a leader they can depend upon.

Q. Now that television has become an important campaign medium, does it mean that the whistle-stop or personal appearance campaign has become less necessary?

A. In my opinion, the whistle-stop and personal appearance campaign is still absolutely necessary because a man is never quite himself on a television program. He can only

be himself when he personally meets people face to face.
Only then can the people fully understand what a man stands
for. In personal appearance, he has to be just himself without the benefit of makeup.

Q. In other words, you get a stimulus from the crowd
and the crowd gets a stimulus from you?

A. That's absolutely true. When a candidate for the
Presidency stands in front of the people, the people get a
chance to analyze his character in a way they can't from
television and radio.

Q. Do you think the people are instinctively better able
to judge a man by looking at him and hearing him in person
than in any other way?

A. That was amply proven in 1948. I don't mean to
boast. I'm just stating a fact.

Q. Do you think that, in the future, men will have to
make as vigorous a campaign for the Presidency as you did
in 1948, strenuous as it was for you?

A. Yes, I do. And that's another reason why I am against
Presidential state primaries, because a man cannot stand two
strenuous campaigns—one to win the state primaries and another to run for election.

Q. You believe, then, that the Presidential state primaries use up a lot of energy and much of the appeal which

should be directed to the public only at the time of an election?

A. I know that from experience because I had to make four campaigns for two Senatorial elections in Missouri, and if I had had to do that on a national basis in 1948, I do not think I could have gone through with it.

Q. As a veteran of many campaigns, which you have continued since you left the White House, do you really enjoy campaigning?

A. Oh, I like it all right. But if I could have my way, I wouldn't do as much of it as I have in the past. It is a very strenuous program for me continually to address large crowds of people, particularly since I have left the White House and no longer have the protection I had as President. For reasons of personal safety, security people maintain a guard over a President, and when he is through talking he can leave without being crushed by enthusiastic and friendly people. I like people and I like to be among them. But take, for instance, a meeting I attended one night at the Muehlebach Hotel in Kansas City. This was quite a few years after I left office. When the meeting was over, I was literally mobbed by the large crowd that was there—and there were a lot of Republicans among them—all of whom wanted autographs. In addition, they wanted to talk to me personally about all sorts of things. They wanted to know what I was going to do and where I had been and how my grandchildren were doing. I just had to struggle to get out of the crowd and out of the place while people nearly pulled my arms out trying to shake my hand. I knew and appreciated what they were trying to say to me, but no man could have stood up to that kind of physical encounter for more than a few minutes. For that reason, whenever it is possible, arrangements now are made for me to get out by a back or side door.

Q. Do you still recall your first speech?

A. Yes, I recall it vividly. It wasn't a speech. It was an exhibition of a thoroughly rattled fellow on the platform who couldn't say a word. This was when I was running for the nomination for the office of eastern judge in Jackson County. The meeting was at Lee's Summit. All the candidates were on the platform. When it was my turn to talk, I was scared to death, and couldn't say anything.

Q. Are you still a little bit nervous every time you approach the platform to make a speech?

A. I certainly am. I am always nervous worrying whether I am properly prepared for what I am going to talk about. You never can be too well prepared when you talk about important matters.

Q. What is your opinion of some of the recent bullying and arrogant labor leaders?

A. Well, I think that eventually they will get their comeuppance. They're just like any other men who get power and get too big for their breeches. The difficulty with these particular leaders is that they've been able to collect too much money. When any man—I don't care who he is—

whether banker, industrialist, labor boss or anybody else—
gets control of too much money, it makes a fool of him, and
that's what's happened to some of the leaders of the Team-
sters Union.

**Q. Is there as much need today for a big labor union as
there used to be?**

A. Yes, I think there is. The labor movement came
through some pretty difficult battles in order to achieve a
measure of economic security for the working man. The
National Labor Relations Act, the Wagner Act, is what put
labor on its feet. As time went on, the act needed amending.
But the Taft-Hartley Act was not the amendment that was
needed, as a lot of people have found out since.

**Q. How do you compare John L. Lewis as a labor leader
to some of those others we have just asked you about?**

A. Well, John L. Lewis was once a fellow who thought
he was kind of a power unto himself. But he found out that
he wasn't, and he adjusted himself to conditions. And another thing—John L. Lewis was honest but the others you
are talking about were not. Lewis fought very hard, and
even sometimes arrogantly, but he always fought for his
people. The others exploited their members for their own
gains.

**Q. What is the best way to protect the union members
from exploitation by labor leaders who misuse union funds
for personal power and benefit?**

A. They should be compelled to make public reports at regular times on what they do with their funds. And dues of the members should be used in a way to accomplish the purposes for which the union was set up. What is more important, these union dues should never be used to create large funds for the personal benefit of the heads of the union.

Q. What do you think about union members being assessed for contributions to political activities?

A. I don't believe in the assessment of dues for political purposes. If the individual members voluntarily contribute to a political party, that's their privilege. But when somebody forces them to throw money into a pot for the use of the leaders of the union, that's wrong. It's absolutely wrong. I don't believe in that and never have, and the less you have to do with political money the better off you are. I never would handle it. I was able to get along all right. Most of the time I didn't have any funds—but I won.

Q. We were going to ask you whether you thought that all labor unions could eventually become more democratic in their set-up and in their relations with their members.

A. Of course, that's what has to be done, because you can't have a dictatorship in labor any more than you ought to have it in industry or in government. In industry we have been trying to stop it by law. In government we are always watchful. And in labor unions, we must arrange matters so that the ordinary fellow who makes up and supports the union has a voice in its operations.

Q. Do you think there's a chance of a labor party similar to the one in Britain evolving in the United States?

A. No, I don't. At least I hope that won't happen. There is no need for a third party, since our two-party system has made our country strong and politically responsive. All segments of our economy and society have adequate representation and expression within either or both parties. Traditionally, of course, the Democratic party has been on the side of labor.

Q. Why is it that a President has so much difficulty deciding on a successor?

A. The principal reason is that we live in a republic, and it's not really the prerogative of the President to decide on his successor, unless he wants to support a man he thinks will carry on his program. In a monarchy, of course, the oldest son, the oldest daughter or whoever happens to be in line of succession takes over when the time comes. But under our form of government, a President has no more right, theoretically, to select his successor than any other man in the government. The convention usually takes care of that.

Q. Didn't you have some difficulty in 1952 in finding someone suitable to succeed you, and didn't Franklin Roosevelt on two occasions have the same problem? Isn't it probable that President Roosevelt continued to succeed himself after the second term because he could find no one to carry on the work he started?

A. That may have been true, though I have no way of

knowing. But then, of course, the President of the United States is the head of the party that elected him, and he naturally has some say in the convention when it meets at the end of his term, as to who shall be the nominee. But very few Presidents have ever had any luck obtaining the man they really wanted for their successor. Andrew Jackson succeeded in nominating Martin Van Buren the first time—but after that, the convention took care of that on its own hook.

The same thing has been true of Republican Presidents. They've had little luck naming their successors, except in the case of Theodore Roosevelt when he named William Howard Taft. And then, when Taft didn't go along with him, Roosevelt fell out with Taft, splitting the Republican party, which led to the nomination and election of Woodrow Wilson. Incidentally, this was one of the finest things that ever happened to the country. So maybe a situation of this kind can turn out for the welfare of the people. You can't tell. No President can really select his successor, although most of them—being in control of the party machinery—try to do it. Sometimes, as with Theodore Roosevelt, they're woefully disappointed with what they've done.

Q. Doesn't it take a special kind of training to qualify for the Presidency today since the United States has become a world leader?

A. Well, that's what a lot of people seem to think, and to a great degree they are right. But if you'll let me boast a little, I think I myself am a fair example of the fact that a special kind of training is not absolutely necessary, if the man has solid experience in government, a knowledge of history and, most important of all, if he does his homework. Granting that a man may possess ability and character, it still is impossible to predict what sort of a President he may turn out to be.

Q. What sort of President have generals made?

A. Some were great, and some were not so great. George Washington was not a professional military man, nor was Andrew Jackson. They both were great Presidents.

Zachary Taylor was the first professional soldier to become President, and he didn't know anything about administration. President William Henry Harrison was another general, but he lived only a month in office. Then we had Ulysses S. Grant, who was distinguished as a general but not as a President. Rutherford B. Hayes, who was a general in the Federal Army in the War Between the States, was a very, very good man who tried his best to be a good President. But he was elected under a cloud because the Democrats charged that the election was stolen—and it probably was. Then the next general to become President was James A. Garfield, who had served in the Federal Army. But he was assassinated a short time after taking office. He was succeeded by Chester Arthur, who was Collector of the Port of New York; you might call him a Republican Tammany politician, but he turned out to be a very good President. The only thing that I ever held against him was that he sold all the fine furniture that Jefferson, Adams and Monroe had brought over from France to furnish the White House. He sold nine van loads of White House furniture at auction for nine thousand dollars.

Chester Arthur was succeeded by Grover Cleveland, who was succeeded by the grandson of another President, Benjamin Harrison. Benjamin Harrison was also a general of the Federal Army. He did not distinguish himself as President.

Q. In this atomic age, how long could we wait to curb a President should he attempt to misuse his power by embarking on some adventure?

A. I don't think we would have to wait at all. First, let me say I don't think we'll ever have a President of that kind. But if we ever do, we always have the power of swift impeachment in the Congress. I shouldn't worry about that because ours is a three-power government that would kick the man on horseback off the horse.

Q. Have you any suggestions as to how we can understand more about American history?

A. I think that the youngsters in our schools and universities should be instructed in the problems of government, but this should be supplemented by some participation by them in the political activities of the community or their neighborhood. They should have an opportunity to see at first hand what goes on in the village and in the city and the county, the state and the nation. All of these operations and administrations are based on the Constitution of the United States. The more our youngsters can become interested in how the government works, from the ground up, the better it will be for the nation and its future. I think you'll find they'll all be interested in doing their part, if they get a chance.

Q. You set up the Hoover-Acheson Commission to conduct a study of the organization of the federal government and to make recommendations for improvement. What do you think has come of it?

A. Very useful and important recommendations for streamlining the government came out of the Hoover-Acheson Commission. Studies of the government organization should be a continuing process. Our country has grown so much that we ought to keep the operation of the government up to date, especially in the executive branch. The executive end of the government is the one that really runs the government, and it should do so without waste or duplication.

Q. Do you read many books, Mr. President?
A. Yes, I read a great deal, but not as much as I want to.

Q. What type of books do you prefer?
A. History and biography. I read all that I can lay my hands on. I sometimes read as many as six books at one time, alternating from one to the other. For example, I received a book about Alexander Hamilton the other day and it was a good one, and I've also been reading one of the best books I have seen on the Civil War—*The Blockade Runners*. I try to keep up with all the new books in history and biography,

but there are so many of them it's hard to keep up with them.

Q. Do you do any light reading?

A. Well, I sometimes read a whodunit. I get most of them sent to me by the publishers or the authors. Erle Stanley Gardner always sends me his latest book, inscribed to me. He used to send them when I was in the White House, and he's kept it up since I came home. Whodunits are a source of recreation to me, but you can get too expert with them. I find that after I have read a few chapters I can tell pretty well how they are going to come out. Roosevelt used to like reading whodunits. He used to begin them, but he seemed to need only a little head start and he could always tell how everything in the book was going to come out. FDR used to like to talk to me about his interest in whodunits.

Q. Do you happen to know whether President Roosevelt did much reading?

A. I don't think I've ever come in contact with anyone who had read more or was more familiar with the history and background of the country than Franklin Roosevelt.

Q. Was he especially interested in things about the sea and the navy?

A. Well, of course he would be. He was Assistant Secretary of the Navy under Wilson. But he was just as interested in all the other activities of the government—as his running of the government, and especially his approach to international affairs, clearly revealed.

Q. Since you were both interested in history, did you ever discuss any particular historians with Mr. Roosevelt?

A. Yes, I did. And we were critical of a few of our contemporary American historians, whose conclusions in some fields we found very inaccurate. Beard was one of the historians we thought had lost his perspective and had gotten too personal in what he had written.

We did on occasion talk about some of the history of the past, the War Between the States and the Napoleonic era. I recall we once talked about the Islamite approach to the conquest of Europe, and how Charles Martel had turned them back at Tours. We discussed such episodes in history as the turning back of the Turks at Vienna, and how Genghis Khan was stopped before he could reach Austria. These were the things we talked about when we were through with our business. Roosevelt was just as interested as I was in history, and knew more about certain phases of it than I did.

Q. We understand you believe that some of the American historians, being New Englanders, were somewhat distorted in their views of certain periods of our history.

A. I think they were, and this is just beginning to come out now. That's the reason why so many books are being written on the Civil War now. The new historians are trying to offset the bias of the New England writers.

Q. Do you object to a historian expressing his personal views?

A. No, not if the historian makes clear that he is expressing his personal views and does not pass off his personal opinions as objective history.

Q. What do you mean by the term "the viewpoint of history" which you have used on several occasions? Is a viewpoint of history a final judgment on all things, and how accurate and dependable is that final judgment?

A. A viewpoint of history is like an editorial—you read it and then reach your own conclusion. The thing that is most important is that history does not become propaganda, misrepresenting the facts of previous generations to the youngsters who are coming on.

Q. Can a man be non-partisan in politics?

A. There never was a non-partisan in politics. A man cannot be a non-partisan and be effective in a political party. When he's in any party he's partisan—he's got to be. The only way a man can act as a non-partisan is when he is in office, either as President or head of a state or county or city. Then he should recognize the fact that there are people on both sides whom he is responsible for and must act for. But when it comes to politics, a man's either one thing or the other.

Q. We understand that you take a special interest in the weather, and that since you left office you get a weather map every day by airmail from Washington.

A. I follow the weather very closely and have done so all my life because I was raised on a farm. I get a weather map daily from Washington, and it is one of the first things I look at in the morning. From these maps I can judge pretty well what sort of weather we can expect for the next few days in all parts of the country. For instance, the weather map I saw this morning showed a low pressure area over northwest Canada that had created a condition causing six inches of snow up there. And then there was a lower pressure area below us, to the southeast. When I arrived at the Library, I saw a line across the northwest sky which indicated to me that a cold wave was going to move in. It did.

Q. Is study of the weather a hobby with you or a point of real interest?

A. It's not only a point of interest, but it means something more to me. When you're on the farm and you have to harvest wheat or sow wheat, or plant corn or gather corn, or decide on what you are going to do with the livestock to be sure that they don't go to town when the weather is cold and lose a lot of weight, you watch the weather all the time. On the farm, I found watching the weather not only necessary but very interesting. And if you watch the birds and the pigs and the cows, you can tell more about what the weather's going to do than the weatherman himself. It is fascinating to watch the antics of the livestock caused by the pressure areas you see on a weather map.

You may be interested to know that George Washington, in his diary, kept track of the temperature and direction of the wind every day. Washington was a farmer, and he found it necessary to watch the weather. But it's surprising to note the extent of the details he recorded.

Thomas Jefferson was just as keenly interested in the weather. Jefferson constructed a weather vane which he patented and installed on Monticello. He had an extension of the weather vane in the shape of a hand inside the house; this showed him the direction of the wind. He also had a measure to gauge the velocity of the wind, which was the forerunner of the wind gauge now in use.

Q. You have talked about Presidents whom you consider great. Can you name some of the Presidents whom you think were not so great?

A. I think maybe I can tell you about some of them without hurting anyone's feelings. We can start with Madison, who was not much of a success as an administrator. He followed Thomas Jefferson, who was one of the greatest of the great Presidents. And you take the man who followed Andrew Jackson, Van Buren. He was one of the best politicians that ever walked but I wouldn't rate him a successful President. When William Henry Harrison died in office, John Tyler was his successor. John Tyler was a Virginian who had been nominated on the Whig ticket. As soon as old William Henry Harrison, who was the head of the Whig ticket, died a month after taking office, Tyler fired all the Whigs and hired Democrats and got into more trouble than you can shake a stick at. Zachary Taylor, who didn't know anything about administration, got into all kinds of troubles. He was a general in the field and won one of the greatest battles of the Mexican War—the Battle of Buena Vista. He gave the famous order to Captain Bragg—"Give them a little more grape, Captain Bragg"—and that won the battle.

Taylor was succeeded in the White House by Millard Fillmore, who was an anti-Mason and a "know-nothing and a do-nothing" President. Fillmore was succeeded by Franklin Pierce from New Hampshire, who signed the bill repealing the Missouri Compromise. This bill was one of the chief contributing factors to the War Between the States. He was absolutely a "do-nothing" President. He'd been a brigadier general in the Mexican War. Whenever there was a big fight on, he took sick.

Pierce was followed by James Buchanan who, I think, was the best example of a "do-nothing" President the United States ever had. President Buchanan could have stopped the Civil War in South Carolina, just as easy as old Jackson did it about twenty years before that. Jackson told South Carolina that if they did not enforce the laws in their state, he'd come down and hang every one of them. And they knew he'd do it.

And that was all that James Buchanan had to do—but he didn't do it.

And then there was Ulysses Grant, who was not only a bad administrator but surrounded himself with people who were even worse administrators. He was followed by Rutherford Hayes, who was a good man and tried his best to pull things out. But Hayes became President on a stolen election and that situation caused him trouble. Well, then, the President who succeeded him was assassinated a short time after he was inaugurated. He was James A. Garfield. Garfield was followed by the best-dressed man—and also the best-looking man—who was ever in the White House, Chester A. Arthur.

He wore sideburns and striped pants with a long coat. Then we had a President a good deal later—but I don't like to get too close to modern times—Harding.

Coolidge, who succeeded on Harding's death, was a Franklin Pierce. He didn't do anything and maybe there wasn't much for him to do. He carried on the government to the extent that was necessary, and he was satisfied with the way things came out. They tell a good story about Coolidge. When he was told about a book "debunking" George Washington, Coolidge turned around, looked out of the window of the White House office, and said: "Well, his monument is still there. I guess it will stand." That's one of the greatest things he ever said.

11

H.S.T.: Roving Teacher (Second Seminar)

I KNOW of no way of communicating more information in a shorter time than the question-and-answer method. There is nothing that stimulates me so much as my sessions with students. I never miss a chance to encourage youngsters to pop questions at me. Here are some further examples of the give-and-take at a typical seminar:

Q. A population explosion is taking place all over the world, including our own country. Have we the resources to meet it?

A. The first thing we must do is to keep on expanding the industrial capacity of this country. Our nation can support a population of 300 million people just as well as the 180 million we now have, providing we manage our resources properly.

Q. What about the rest of the world, especially in those parts that are underdeveloped and are experiencing an even greater percentage of growth of population?

A. That is a big problem, but it can be solved if we all do the things that are necessary to meet this challenge. It is estimated that the population of the world, which is now about two and a half billion people, will go to six or seven billion in ten or fifteen years. We have to meet this situation by a program of development of the resources of all the nations so that all their people can be fed and clothed and have places to live and reproduce if they want to. And the best way to do that is to find a way to utilize the potentially productive areas of the earth that are not now in production. We are now developing practical ways of converting sea water into fresh water, and if we can develop this on a large enough scale we can make gardens out of such places as the Sahara Desert and the Gobi Desert. The soil is there, and all that it needs to be productive is to bring water to it. This can be done and will be done, simply because the pressure of increased population will force it.

Q. Wouldn't this program have to be carried out on an international basis, or can we undertake this on our own initiative in assisting other nations?

A. We cannot and should not undertake this by ourselves. It has to be done on an international basis. Many of the underdeveloped nations are unable to do this for themselves and need help and advice. But there are many problems of sovereignty that have to be solved before we can barge right in. Take, for example, the Sahara Desert. This area is under the control of the Arabs on the east, the French on the north and a number of independent countries in Africa on the south. All will have to get together and agree on a cooperative plan to bring water to this desert. Where would the waters come from for such a project? When we solve the salt water conversion problems, the nations could utilize the inexhaustible water resources of the great seas close by.

And there are other vast areas, such as the Amazon basin of South America. Here, of course, water is not the problem. The need is for scientific agricultural development. This basin alone is capable of supporting a population of three hundred million, where today there are only fifty million people.

Q. Is this part of what you envisaged under your Point Four Program?

A. The over-all purpose of Point Four was to help people to help themselves. In this way they could achieve a higher standard of living in freedom, and all the people would be helped instead of just the few who in the past exploited the masses. The main aim of the Point Four Program, when first suggested, was to make a beginning in providing instruction and assistance to each nation to develop its own resources. In this way, I thought it would make it easier for the world to get along and work together in improving the lot of all people and to meet the needs of the growing population everywhere.

Q. Isn't this the first time in history that a major power had thought of such an undertaking?

A. There has never been a government in the history of the world that has been willing, after winning a war, to rehabilitate its enemies instead of robbing them and killing off their populations and putting them out of business. This is all the more significant when you consider that we were thrust into the war by mad dictators who sought to conquer the world. After we came out victorious, we did our best, not only to help our friends and allies but to help our enemies as well. We even wanted to do more than that, hating war as we do and realizing that economic strains and stresses were factors leading to wars. We sought to do everything we could to encourage economic betterment throughout the world by international participation and self-help.

Q. What is your concept of the role of America in the world?

A. Well, I think of the government of the United States as the greatest government in the history of the world. Its continuation is absolutely essential to the welfare and benefit of all people who would be free. Our first duty is to maintain our own freedom and to work for the freedom of all nations throughout the world.

Q. How do you define an American? We talk about a Frenchman, we talk about an Englishman, a Russian or a German. What's an American?

A. Well, I don't like to call a citizen of the United States, or a citizen of any of the other republics in the Western Hemisphere, an American. The citizens of the United States are a mixture out of the melting pot. They are made up of all the races of Europe and other parts of the world, and they have come out with a generation that I think is better than any other generation that ever came about. Now, if you want to talk about one hundred per cent Americans, you must go back to the inhabitants of the United States at the time that European settlers first landed in Massachusetts, in Virginia, in Georgia, in South Carolina and in North Carolina. These inhabitants were North Americans.

Columbus thought he had discovered India and that is the way they came to be called Indians. They were the one hundred per cent Americans. You'll find that some of the greatest patriots in the history of the world were those Indian leaders who fought for the welfare of their people against the European invaders of the North American continent. I think we treated the Indians badly. We murdered as many as we could, and took their land away from them. I have always felt that the Indians should have been allowed to maintain themselves on the lands and improve their position, and eventually they would have become friendly to us. They had the same sort of brains and body as we have, and they are a brave people.

And let us not forget that, long before the European invaders penetrated the North American and South American continents, there were two great civilizations in Peru and Mexico. They were among the greatest civilizations the world has ever known, particularly the Incas in Peru.

Q. How do you feel about self-designated groups who refer to themselves as one hundred per cent Americans?

A. I think some of them get out of line, especially when they develop a little social superiority complex about their ancestors. One of the best things I ever heard was when Will Rogers boasted of his ancestors. He was addressing a meeting of the Daughters of the American Revolution. He told them he was glad to see so many badges on them indicating that their ancestors were in the American Revolution. They had been telling him how many were descended from Colonial people who were way up in the economic scale, and that they were among the first to land on American shores. Will Rogers said he was very happy that was the case because his ancestors were there to meet them. Will Rogers, you know, was part Indian.

Q. Mr. President, what is it you think of when you think of America? Englishmen—when they talk of England—so often wax poetic about the beauty of England.

A. I think of America always in terms of people—people who are making this country what it is. I think it's wonderful to have beautiful scenery, and we have some of the most beautiful anywhere, particularly here in Missouri. But it is people who make the country. And when I think of America I think of Americans, who are the most generous people in the world. Whatever troubles or problems we face as a nation, I don't think there's anything to worry about regarding the heart of the American people, because it's right. We've taken the Irish, the Italians, the Jews, the Poles, the

English and the French and the Germans, the Russians, and the Swedes, the Norwegians, the Danes and the Greeks— and men and women from all parts of Europe and the world. And we've put them together, and they are all Americans. If you go back at least two or three generations, you'll find that the grandparents or great grandparents came from some country on the other side of the Atlantic, and you can't tell the youngsters of the present day from the Americans whose ancestors came to these shores three hundred or four hundred years ago.

Q. What future do you see for the Republican party?

A. Well, they've got to find a program that will do what they tried to do in 1852 and in 1856. They've got to find a program that will be in the best interests of all the people of the country. But I think they're looking in the wrong direction. They won't find it on Wall Street—or even on Madison Avenue.

Q. Could business and management continue their support of the Republican party if that party took up the cause of labor or of the little man whom the Democrats have always represented?

A. Well, that would probably be a good thing. That would be a good thing because then management and business would find out that the people who work for them, in a free republic where a man can vote for what or whom he pleases, are their best assets for their own success.

Q. Does the United States need its two-party system?

A. Yes, it does. You've got to have a two-party system in order to have an opposition to keep those in control on their toes. If you don't, the first thing you know, the top dog will forget the underdog, as the underdog sometimes does when he becomes the top dog. That's the human animal.

Q. Do you think the South is a drag on the Democratic party?

A. I think the South is coming around to where it ought to be. You see, the Southern bloc was brought about by the situation after the War Between the States. This situation arose from the Reconstruction Program, and a great many people in the South had a terrible time getting over their feeling about the North. My mother and father never did get over it, but I know that the best thing for the world, and for the United States, was what Lincoln did to make a nation out of this country. And we are gradually convincing the southerners that that was the best thing for them too, although, like my mother, they don't like Lincoln, Grant or Sherman!

Q. Do you think there is an important future for the South?

A. There isn't any doubt about it in my mind. The southerners are just as fine a people as you will find anywhere in the nation. And when they come to the conclusion that race and creed and color don't make any difference in what's in a man's heart, then we won't have any trouble.

Q. **Are you of the opinion, Mr. Truman, that there is sign of a change taking place in the South?**

A. I believe there is, and I believe a gradual change has been taking place all along. You will recall that I left no doubt where I stood on the important issues involving the South in my campaign of 1948. I took a stand which involved serious political risks, and some of the southern states "seceded" from the Democratic party. But there was no other course that we could follow and keep the Bill of Rights a living thing. Despite the recent resurgence of stubborn sectionalism and racism on the part of some extremists, I believe the South is heading in the right direction.

Q. **Haven't there been prominent members of both parties taking independent positions who have made important contributions to the country?**

A. Yes, there have been, particularly in the United States Senate. When you go into history, you discover that there have been some very great men who, even though they took a minority stand, kept striving for legislation for the welfare of the people. And they kept at it—even though they were being voted down on their proposals—because they felt they were right. Take George Norris, senator from Nebraska. The Tenessee Valley Authority is a monument to his foresight, courage and persistence. Because of him, public power became one of our great national assets. Senator Bob LaFollette, Sr., of Wisconsin is another man who made a great contribution to our forward progress, as did his son Bob when he took his place in the United States Senate. But just think! They were succeeded by a Joe McCarthy. How are you going to account for that? It seems people eventually get weary of strong and dynamic men like Norris and LaFollette, regardless of their great contributions, and vote in their extreme opposites just for a change.

Q. Do you think then that the country can take just so much progress at a time and then it demands a change?
A. That's right. Every now and then the country seems to take a "breather." And the people usually pay a terrible price for it. The nation came out of a war under the great leadership of Woodrow Wilson, tired of the strain and sacrifice. The people were offered "normalcy" under Harding—and they took it. This period of "normalcy" led up to the great panic of 1929. Then came Franklin Roosevelt with a dynamic New Deal program of social reforms and eventually things got back on the track.

Q. Do you think people also get tired of forward-looking Presidents and Presidents who get them out of trouble?
A. Yes, they do.

Q. Do you think they were getting tired in 1948?
A. A great many of the people, mostly Republicans, assumed that the people were tired of sixteen years of Roosevelt and Truman. But I was sure they were wrong. I traveled up and down the country and saw for myself. I kept my eyes open, as well as an ear to the ground, although I remembered what Hanna said about McKinley. He said that he

had his ears so close to the ground that he had them full of grasshoppers. But my hearing didn't get impaired.

Q. President Truman, is it your opinion that the Democratic party is keeping pace with the times?
A. Oh, I'm sure of that. The Democratic party is the only party that has lasted for over a hundred years. And it's getting stronger. The Democratic party must continue to stay on the side of the little fellow.

Q. Was the election and re-election of President Eisenhower a Republican party victory or a personal victory?
A. It was a personal victory, of course.

Q. Some people suggest that you are getting mellowed and less militant. Is that so?
A. Not in the slightest degree. They are trying to make an elder statesman of me but they will never succeed.

Q. Can we ask you, Mr. President, whether you think this nation is providing adequate medical care for the people?
A. Well, public health is a peculiar situation. You see, the scientists have discovered ways to control nearly all the plagues mankind has suffered from. New medicines, such as antibiotics and a host of new drugs and new scientific equipment, are making it possible not only to cure people but to prolong human life. But the cost for the ordinary

person to get proper treatment is almost prohibitive for people in the middle and lower income brackets. The very rich can afford them. The very poor are taken care of by welfare organizations and institutions. The man in the middle, who is the biggest taxpayer, cannot meet the situation when members of his family have to go to the hospital and stay there.

The way to solve that problem is to build up a backlog of funds with which to pay the hospitals and the doctors. A government program is needed to raise the necessary funds. This could be done through a small addition to our present social security tax on salaries and wages, divided between the employer and employee. That doesn't mean that the government will control it when the people pay in their money for this medical insurance. The fund will be established so that every person can meet his medical costs without anyone becoming a charity case. And every patient will have a perfect right to decide on the doctor and hospital of his choice. This is a plan in the best American tradition. To criticize it as socialistic is silly. And one thing is certain. Opponents of such a program—mostly, I am afraid, the representatives of organized medicine who have managed so far to block enactment of necessary legislation—will not be able to prevent its eventual adoption. Whether they like it or not, the people who are affected by the high cost of medicine and hospitalization have the most votes.

Q. Is it correct, Mr. Truman, that you once suggested sending medical missionaries around the world?

A. Yes, I have had in mind for a long time the idea of

sending doctors and nurses as medical missions to help the areas of the world which do not now have adequate medical facilities. I realize that we ourselves need more doctors and nurses to take care of our own sick, and I therefore think we ought to have a kind of crash program to train doctors and nurses in such large numbers that we can meet not only the need here but also the need in other areas of the world.

Q. Is it true that some of the people in the Roosevelt Administration did not take too kindly to you at first when you became President?

A. Yes, it's true. There was some of that, but it is only to be expected when there is a sudden change. I took little notice of it because I understood exactly how people who were close to Roosevelt felt. They had lost their leader and they were down in the dumps. They were probably afraid that the country would go to the dogs with a new man whom they thought didn't know much about what to do. But after they found out—that is, the vast majority of them —that I was going to carry out the policies and ideals of Franklin Roosevelt to their logical conclusion, they began to feel differently. I never held a grudge against any of them, not even those who were indiscreet enough to voice their misgivings or disapproval of me publicly.

Q. Why have so few senators or congressmen been called to the Presidency?

A. The main difficulty in the selection of a man to run for President from the Congress is the fact that, if he has been an active member of the Senate or the House of Representatives, he has committed himself on all the great issues that are before the country. You take the governors of great states, they don't have to do that. Their main concern is carrying out their responsibilities of local government. They are usually not called on to make statements on national or international issues. Nor do they have to vote for the record on any issues that the people of the country as a whole are interested in. That's why governors are more often sought out by both parties to be candidates for the Presidency.

Q. In other words, if today you say some Senator or Congressman is supposed to have no strong views on any important or controversial issues, the best thing to do is to look at his voting record.

A. That is correct. What a member of Congress may say publicly is one thing. How he votes is another.

Q. Has the Cabinet ever been a steppingstone for the Presidency?

A. No, the Cabinet has not been a good jumping off place for the Presidency, except in the early days of the Republic. In recent times, we have had only one example—Herbert Hoover, who was Secretary of Commerce before he became President.

Q. Why is it that we don't hear or read more about the Chief Justices of the United States and the outstanding Associate Justices of the Supreme Court?

A. For the same reason that we haven't heard enough about some of our Presidents. The only reason we know so much about Chief Justice Marshall is that Senator Beveridge of Indiana took a personal interest in him and wrote a biography of him, which made him better known. But I understand that the present Chief Justice is now trying to have something worked out so that biographies of every Chief Justice and Associate Justice from 1789 to date will be written and eventually published. We will then find out a great many things about Justices of the Court that we are not now familiar with because, up to now, it has been a neglected subject.

Q. How do you account for the fact that the members of an impartial body like the Supreme Court, which is presumed to judge on the basis of law, take such opposite views, one seemingly conservative and the other liberal?

A. Well, that's part of our system of government. Both of our political parties in our two-party system are made up of all shades of thought, from conservative to liberal, and that's good for the country. And the arguments that the Justices conduct in the course of arriving at their decisions is a part of a process that is beneficial to the country.

Q. Is the Constitution, Mr. President, a conservative or a liberal document?

A. It is both. It depends on the interpretation. It took the Court a long time to find those words in the Constitution which made it a liberal document. On the other hand,

throughout our history, there were some Justices who took
the view that the Constitution was written for the benefit
of special privilege. But by trial and experience we managed to find out what was right for the country. And that's
the way it should be. You couldn't have had this freedom of
interpretation if you had somebody whose final word is law.

Q. Was the Constitution conceived to be flexible so that
it could adjust itself to the times, or did it happen to work
out that way?

A. I think it worked out that way. I think that the intention of the men who wrote the Constitution was to have
a document that would be a lasting instrument of government. But I don't think they had any more idea than we
have today of what the future will bring forth and how the
Constitution was to work out. So far it has worked out to be
one of the greatest documents of government that ever was
written. The men who wrote it profited from their knowledge of previous governments in history, and their objective
was to set up a free government with checks and balances
so that no one man could get control and turn himself into a
dictator.

Q. There have been many feelings expressed recently
that the Supreme Court is encroaching on the prerogative
of the legislature and the legislature, in turn, is trying to
curb the Supreme Court. How do you feel about Congress
passing legislation deliberately designed to override the
opinions of the Court?

A. The legislative branch cannot curb the Supreme Court as it is set up in the Constitution. And it would take a constitutional amendment for Congress to curb the Supreme Court. Congress should never have the right, categorically, to override the decisions of the Court. If you give Congress the authority to override the Court in the decisions that they make, you won't have a free Supreme Court.

Q. President Truman, do you think that taxes are going still higher? Are the people going to stand for it?

A. As long as we have to face a world situation that challenges our security, and as long as we have to continue in an armaments race, we cannot expect and certainly we cannot afford lower taxes. But I believe that our tax structure needs to be completely restudied and streamlined, because it has become cumbersome, overlapping and, in many instances, inequitable. Even as far back as the time when I was presiding judge of the county court of Jackson County, I wrote that the tax burden ought to be borne in such a way that every section of the government, local, state and national, would have its own source of tax revenue without encroaching on the other.

I think a good solution to the problem would be something along this line: The federal government should derive all of its revenue from taxation on income, personal and corporate. The state government should get all of its revenue from a sales tax. Local, city and county governments should be allowed to tax only real estate—that is, land and improvements, and perhaps personal property. The trouble is that today the federal government, the state government, and cities and communities within the state, are competing to tax the same sources for revenue. This cannot go on, and in many cases, in state and local governments, we are reaching a point of no return. Some communities have already reached a critical stage where the voters are rejecting school bonds and other essential financing for community services.

Q. Can you tell us what you mean by competition in taxation?

A. Well, you have the state imposing a sales tax for the building of roads. You have the federal government levying a gasoline tax for the building of highways. You have the state and the federal government levying an income tax. It is getting very difficult for local governments to find places to tax in order to get the money to run their governments. Let me add that there are many loopholes in our existing structure of federal taxation which ought to be plugged up so that we can give the lower income people some relief. We also ought to consider streamlining many government operations on all levels to wipe out senseless and costly duplication.

Q. Mr. President, during your Administration you had a major problem trying to fuse the military forces into a working unit. Didn't Congress want to go along on the plan?

A. No, they didn't.

Q. Is it still your feeling that there should be a tighter amalgamation of the armed forces?

A. There isn't a doubt in the world but that the whole thing ought to be tightened up so that the President, as commander-in-chief, could deal through a Secretary of Defense who should have direct control of the defenses of the nation—just as the Secretary of War did when George Washington set up the first defense program. Before making my recommendations to Congress, I had correspondence with every single commanding general in the field—a stack of correspondence a yard high. I don't know whether it's been destroyed or not. All of the opinion was that the Secretary of Defense should have this control under direct orders of the President, and without interference from the separate secretaries of the separate services who keep getting in one another's way. The Secretary of War under Washington had control of the army and navy and marines. Then the eager beavers of the navy got separated from the Secretary of War, and we had a Secretary for the Navy. That was the first split, and then finally we got the Air Force and a separate Secretary for Air. We need to get the idea over that the Defense Department of the Government of the United States is of vital importance and must not be tampered with by conflicting forces. It ought to operate under direct control of a man who knows where he's going and why. He should be the Secretary of Defense in complete control of all the services, ground, sea and air, under the direction of the Commander-in-Chief—the President of the United States.

12

What Happens to a President's Family

I HAVE sometimes wondered whether a President ought to have any descendants when I see how complicated their lives are made by their connection with the White House. Of course, in the case of my own family, I feel that I have been the luckiest of men so far, and I hope the future will be as kind.

Throughout our history, it has been a very difficult situation for the descendants of Presidents, because so many people insist on regarding them as if they were the offspring of hereditary rulers; they are expected to be out of the ordinary and to maintain a special prominence. It seems that, even in a republic where people vest authority in a President, they want to glamorize not only him but his family.

I feel that the descendants of Presidents are entitled to be treated just as any citizens. And they ought to have the same chance to make their own way. There have been instances where the kin of Presidents have tried to capitalize on their relationship—to the embarrassment of their families. But in the main, the nation may well be proud of the restraint and modesty which has characterized the behavior of the descendants of those who occupied the White House.

Without any prompting by me, my own daughter Margaret and my nieces and nephews have pursued their own lives and not one of them has presumed on his or her connection with the man in the White House.

But it has been a problem, not only for the direct offspring of a President but even for his collateral descendants—the brothers and sisters, and cousins as well, who have had their difficulties and harassments in trying to live their own lives.

The biggest handicap children of a President face is the pitiless publicity they have to suffer when they happen to make a mistake—and they make no more mistakes than the children of other citizens. My sympathy is with them, because they are always in the limelight whether they want it or not.

That is why I never have been severely critical of the children of any President, no matter what was said about them nor or how they became involved in the headlines. And even long after their parents leave the White House, they cannot escape attention.

People try to promote them for their own welfare and benefit. And politicians try the same thing because, when a man makes a name in the Presidency, that name becomes a political asset to be exploited. All manner of people are trying to involve these sons and daughters of Presidents in doing things that they ought not do.

The offspring of the Presidents have no special obligations or privileges and should have none in a republic. They must make their own way in life. But even the relatives of Presidents, three or four times removed, do not altogether escape the limelight.

My brother has four boys and a daughter, and my sister is a very close member of the family. She never married because she stayed with our mother until her death at ninety-four. But all of these members of my family were constantly in the public eye against their will, and the limelight was aimed at them for the purpose of finding something wrong— not something right.

But no one ever found anything wrong with them. Not a single member of my family or the family of Mrs. Truman ever embarrassed me in any way as President of the United States. I hope they can say the same about me.

It must have been a terrific strain on all of them because it did not make any difference what they did, even if they just turned around on the street, some reporter had something to say about it. But in the years since I returned home, I have not had one single moment of embarrassment from any of them, and I am as happy as I can be about that.

Whenever relatives of the President seek to go into business or politics they are accused of taking advantage of their special relationship. This has been so from the very beginning of our Republic. Take the embarrassment of the second President of the United States, John Adams, who was concerned about what would be said if he reappointed his son, John Quincy Adams, to a foreign mission. John Quincy Adams had been appointed Minister to Holland by George Washington and had served at his post with great brilliance.

Turning for advice to George Washington, Adams inquired whether it would be proper upon succeeding to the Presidency for him to retain his son in the foreign service. Washington, replying, wrote: "If my wishes would be of any avail, they should go to you in a strong hope that you will not withhold merited promotion from Mr. John Adams because he is your son. For without intending to compliment the father and the mother, or to censure any others, I give it as my decided opinion that Mr. Adams is the most valuable public character we have abroad—and that he will prove himself to be the ablest of all our diplomatic corps. If he was now to be brought into that line or into any other public walk, I could not, upon the principle which has regulated my own conduct, disapprove a caution which is hinted at in the letter. But he is already entered; the public more and more, as he is known, are appreciating his talents and work; and his country would sustain a loss if these are checked by over delicacies on your part."

The fact that John Quincy Adams was the son of a President raised a question about the propriety of his appointment which would not have been raised about any other person. And had the second President not received encouragement from George Washington, we might well have lost the talents and services of John Quincy Adams, the man who was to be one of the great architects of American foreign policy.

In writing to her son, John Quincy, Abigail, the wife of

John Adams, cautioned him not to expect any appointment from his father when he became President.

John Quincy, replying to his mother, said: "I hope my dear and honored mother . . . that I shall never give him any trouble by solicitation for office of any kind."

I find it unfair, too, to compare the children of Presidents to their fathers, because they rarely have the opportunity of achieving the office of President themselves, and there is very little chance of their being considered for it. There have been only two families in which two members of each were President of the United States. They were the Adams and Harrison families.

Only once in our history has one man been the son of a President and the father of another President. He was John Scott Harrison, son of the ninth President, William Henry Harrison, and the father of the twenty-third President, Benjamin Harrison.

More recently the families of Roosevelt—both branches —and the Tafts have been politically prominent. In the case of the Roosevelts, cousins were involved, and Senator Taft never had the chance to follow in his father's footsteps. Robert Taft, I think, was an exception to the general pattern of the son being handicapped by a father who was President. He had stature in his own right, and became a powerful leader in the United States Senate, where he displayed genuine ability and strong independent views.

I find myself somewhat puzzled by the acts of the sons of President Millard Fillmore and Abraham Lincoln, both of whom tried to burn all the private papers of their fathers. Robert Lincoln (the son of Abraham Lincoln), who was President of the Pullman Company, was discovered one day

burning his father's papers in New Hampshire when he was
visited by Nicholas Murray Butler, president of Columbia
University. Butler tried to stop him, but unfortunately he
was able to save only a few of the letters and papers. The
great bulk of them, including correspondence between Lincoln and his wife, were lost forever to history.

I have come to the conclusion that Fillmore's son, as
well as the son of Abraham Lincoln, were rather ashamed of
the origins of their fathers and wanted to be sure that anything indicating that they did not come of aristocratic or
distinguished beginnings should be destroyed. That, of
course, is my own opinion.

No papers or letters of a President should be destroyed,
for none is too trivial or too personal but that it reveals something to future historians of a President's character and
thoughts. I have placed a part of our family letters in the
Library for future use by historians. These letters are in the
Truman Library to be studied at the proper time and under
the proper circumstances after our passing.

IF people were more familiar with American history I think
they would be a little more considerate of the President's
family. I have often thought that those Presidents who did
not have any children suffered less embarrassment in certain things than those that did have them.

And the wives of some Presidents have come in for their
share of gossip and unjust criticism. I do not think there was
anyone in the whole history of our country as unmercifully
treated as Mrs. Abraham Lincoln. She was, in fact, persecuted

and vilified, and I do not think there were ever any grounds for these attacks on her. It only made matters more difficult for the President and distorted the real issues and objectives of his Administration.

All in all, though, most of the Presidents' wives have been more respectfully treated than their husbands. I hope some day someone will take time to evaluate the true role of the wife of a President, and to assess the many burdens she has to bear and the contributions she makes.

The White House is not a home but a temporary residence, and it takes a great deal of talent and work on the part of the President's wife to make it livable. Making it livable makes it possible for the President to carry out his heavy burdens. The White House is a difficult place to raise a family, and the environment is not always a normal atmosphere for an American child.

Since leaving the White House, I have thought more and more about how much the privacy of the President and his family is invaded by the security and formal requirements of the Presidency. How often I felt it was too bad that our own temporary occupancy of the White House had resulted in a permanent compromise of our privacy.

13

Reflections
of a Grandfather

ONE very important event in our lives after our return home was the marriage of our daughter Margaret to Clifton Daniel, Jr.

Margaret's future happiness and welfare were naturally always uppermost in our minds. And when she decided on the man she wanted to marry, Mrs. Truman and I were happy and hopeful that he would be the sort of man we thought Margaret ought to have. And it turned out just that way.

When Margaret lived at the White House she was subject to rumors and speculation of romance. This has been the experience of all marriageable daughters who have lived there. Newspapers and magazines seemed constantly busy trying to link Margaret with some mythical suitor. Even a casual date was a subject for gossip by the columnists. And when Margaret married Clifton, after we had left the White

House, we were happy that it was a real love affair between both of them.

We are a close-knit family, and we keep in daily touch by telephone no matter where we happen to be. Margaret had often talked to us about Clifton. Yet when Margaret broke the news to us of their decision to marry, I was just as surprised as all fathers, I suppose, must be.

We are happy and delighted with our son-in-law, and with his family. The wedding ceremony was simple, since Margaret and Clifton and both families wanted it to be that way. It took place in Independence on April 21, 1956.

That was a day we will always remember. And we were all glad that our wishes for privacy were respected by the press. By now we have become accustomed to the fact that we no longer have complete privacy in our lives.

THE birth, on June 5, 1957, of a first grandson, Clifton Truman Daniel, brought new joy into our lives. I had always wanted a son and now we had a grandson.

Our happiness was compounded with the birth of a second grandson, William Wallace Daniel, who came May 19, 1959.

Wherever I go, people ask me all sorts of personal questions about my grandchildren, and I know this is their way of expressing their good will and interest in me and my family. I get many letters giving me advice on how my grandchildren should be brought up. But more often, those who take the trouble to write ask how I intend to raise my grandchildren.

This is what I try to tell them: I do not think grand-parents should interfere in the business of raising grand-children when the parents are perfectly capable of doing it. These grandchildren of ours have a good father and a good mother who are doing a fine job now and who will know how to raise their children as the years add new responsi-bilities. Parents cannot do what they have to do if they get undue interference from their "ancestors." We are not going to meddle.

And I hope, as our grandsons grow, they will be able to adjust themselves to conditions as they go along. If ever they try to impress people with the fact that they happen to be descendants of a man who has been in the White House, I know what their father and mother will say, and I am certain the boys will come out all right. I do not think anyone will have to worry on that score. On the contrary, the very opposite question concerns me.

As I have often said, I do not know whether Presidents ought to have any descendants, because their descendants inherit the difficult burden of having people expect them to live up to their ancestor. In a sense, a special handicap is imposed upon them. We are a democracy and have no privi-leged classes with hereditary distinctions. Yet people too often look at descendants of Presidents in a way that sets them apart from others and makes unwarranted demands on them.

They ought not do that. Such descendants ought to be treated just as any other citizens. They should be able to make their own way normally, the same as do the children of other people. I hope my grandsons will have that chance as they grow to manhood. One thing I expect will help my grandsons is the fact that their name is somewhat different from their Grandfather Truman's name, and for that reason they are not likely to experience as much trouble as they otherwise might.

THE most persistent questions asked me about my grandsons fall into these categories: What special advice have I for them? Do I want them to go into politics and public life? What should their education be? Should they live in small towns or big cities? What kind of a world are they going to live in?

I have had enough experience in all my years, and have read enough of the past, to know that advice to grandchildren is usually wasted. If the second and third generations *could* profit by the experiences of the first generation, we would not be having some of the troubles we have today.

Each generation thinks it is wiser than the previous one. A lot of youngsters insist they are smarter than their ancestors, and therefore, having thrown out a good deal of what had been previously achieved, they try to start out on their own. They soon find that they have to go through an experience similar, in basic human terms, to the previous generation's.

Yet I never give up hope that young people will some day accept more readily the experience of the past as a starting point and go on to enlarge the scope of human achievement. And I am never more reassured than when I talk to the young college boys and girls and see how eager they are to know the past. And this is what I usually talk about to them.

Specifically, I would like to think that my grandsons will be educated in reading, writing, arithmetic and then the higher mathematics and the basic sciences so essential to the knowledge of the expanding world. They ought to have a knowledge of Latin and Greek, and some foreign language currently spoken. I think they should know ancient and modern history and, most important, the history of the United States, which can be better understood against the background of world history.

Most of my own ideas on how the world runs I obtained very early in life from the Bible, the King James version of the Old and the New Testaments. The Bible is, among other things, one of the greatest documents of history. Every trouble that humanity is heir to is set out in the Bible. And the remedy is there, too, if you know where to find it. I read the Bible at least a dozen times, and maybe more, before I was fifteen years old. The Bible must be read over and over again to get the full meaning out of it. The same is true of the Constitution of the United States.

And the moral code that is in the Old and New Testaments is needed by all mankind. If civilization is to continue, the majority of the people of the world must have a moral code by which to live, and by which to act. The moral code set forth in the Bible is unequalled. Of course, these youngsters in whom I am so vitally interested will be brought up on a moral code, I hope, based on the great code of the Old and New Testaments.

As to what my grandsons are going to do when their basic education is completed, that is something about which

they will have to make up their own minds. I may as well
say that, since they will anyway. Whether they eventually
go into business or finance, or run a farm, or go into any
other occupation or career, that will be up to them. But the
background knowledge of what has been accomplished before, in whatever specific field they enter, is absolutely essential if they are to be successful.

I would like to see them take part in public life, whether
by devoting part of their time while pursuing another pro-
fession or career, or by giving full time to public service.
But that especially is something that they should decide for
themselves, for I think it would be wrong to try to influence
them just because their grandfather was once in the White
House.

As I have been telling the young people I often talk to,
I think every boy in a republic should have some military
service. I tried to get into military service before I was
twenty-one, but could not do so because my mother and
father were unreconstructed southerners, and they were
afraid I would have to wear a blue uniform.

Yet a blue uniform is what I did wear when I became
a member of the National Guard of Missouri at twenty-one.
I was a private in Battery "B" of the First Battalion Field
Artillery of the Missouri National Guard. At that time pri-
vates had to pay twenty-five cents a day to drill.

Every young man who is a citizen of a republic must be
willing to do his part in defending it when it is in danger.
If he has preliminary military training, he is in a better position to do his duty. Anyone who is not willing to fight for
his country is not of much use to the republic.

George Washington, in his first message to Congress,

recommended that we have a well-trained militia. What he meant was that we have a citizen army and not a professional one. If every citizen is trained in military service and then resumes private life, he is always better able not only to join in helping to protect the country but also to make sure that we always have civilian supremacy over the military. Where the professional military are in control of a government or a political set-up, there is always danger of dictatorship.

When, in ancient times, the citizens of Rome themselves fought and did not depend upon mercenary armies, Rome was at its height as a republic. When a professional military class took over, Rome got into the hands of the Emperors, and the decline of Roman might began with dependency on mercenaries. Today, military training in our country is not merely for defense purposes but is also very useful in the development of self-discipline and the ability to organize and get along with other people.

I FIND that when people talk to me about my grandsons they sometimes start by asking why I prefer to live in the country or in a small town. I answer that I prefer the small town because you know everybody and his connections, and you know his sisters and his cousins and his aunts. When you live in a big town, you get to know very few people. It is almost the same as living in the desert.

And what is the advantage of knowing everybody in a town? Well, people are always more friendly in a town, and they can always give you advice when you need it. And neighbors are ready to help neighbors when they are in trouble.

When I talk like that I am sure to get the comment: "But still, *your* grandchildren are being brought up in the big city of New York." Well, I think time will take care of that.

Above all, I want my grandsons to have a normal and healthy life, and as they grow up I hope they will not believe that material success is the important thing. I do not want them to consider that the accumulation of property and money is the main thing in life. Of course, they must have enough to live on and I am sure they will have the ability to achieve that. But while they are doing that, if they should be more successful than other people, they ought not to forget how they arrived where they are. And I hope they will never be unmindful of the people who are not so successful. In a republic such as ours, people must be willing to see to it that every section of the population is as well treated as they hope to be themselves.

I believe that one of the most important conditioners for a real democrat with a small "d" is for him to be at some time or other exposed to adversity. It has been my experience that if a man does not suffer adversity, he never appreciates what it is like for people who do suffer it. When a fellow has been through adversity he is more likely to have a kindlier feeling than those who have never been through trouble.

I think the world in which my grandsons will be growing up will be much more interesting and exciting than the one in which our grandfathers lived. I wish I could live fifty years more to see how everything comes out. Of course, the most important question confronting the generation of my grandsons is whether they, too, are going to be involved in war.

With the new methods of destruction, the possibility of any kind of war is a terrifying prospect. We have to face the fact that two of the most frightful wars in history were fought within recent times. No one can predict with certainty what will happen in the future. Man will have to learn how to save himself from destruction, and one nation by itself cannot abolish wars. Good courageous leaders and statesmen will be needed more than ever.

And I hope my grandson's generation will produce them.

I MUST confess I behaved like a doting grandfather when our two grandchildren spent their first Christmas with us in Independence in 1959. There was no question as to who was in charge. They were.

I took young Clifton by the hand and he led me everywhere he wanted to go. As I took him through the Library, he directed me to what he wanted to see. The things that fascinated him were the shiny things. He lingered longest over the exhibition of the jeweled sword which Ibn Saud, King of Saudi Arabia, had sent me, and which I had turned over to the Library.

Clifton showed that he had a mind of his own and was as stubborn as his grandfather—and his father and his mother. Stubbornness is a helpful trait, if you put it to good use. If you carry it too far it usually spells trouble.

Whenever young Clifton saw any pictures of people in uniform, he would exclaim: "Parade, parade."

I think he is going to like parades.

And when he saw, on the grounds of the Library, the replica of the Liberty Bell, which had been presented to the people of Independence by the people of Annecy-le-Vieux, Haute Savoie, France, he made me unblock the clapper so that he could sound off.

Eventually, I had to drag him away.

Clifton looks like his father. His brother William, of course, was not old enough to get around, and spent most of his time in the crib or in the arms of his grandmother and his mother and his grandfather. He seemed happy. He looks like his mother.

But no matter whom the boys look like, it is going to be wonderful to watch them grow.

14

Six Great Decisions
in Our History

Some scholars of American history with whom I talk from time to time are of the opinion that it is history that makes the man. I am inclined to differ. I think that it is the man who makes history. I find that throughout our own history the greatest strides occur when courageous and gifted leaders either seize the opportunity or create it.

Since 1953, I have been rereading the lives of each of our Presidents, and in the light of my own experience, I have been better able to understand many momentous events and decisions.

We have had some glorious moments in our history—and some dark and difficult periods. Many of the important advances we have made as a nation have come during the administrations of strong Presidents. There are certain events that were milestones in our path, events that helped to make us a great republic and a leader in the free world.

A government may be organized under the highest ethical ideals. On paper, it may sound efficient. Yet the real test of any government is: how authoritatively can it govern?

I have picked out some historic decisions made by six Presidents that illustrate the influence strong leaders have had in shaping events.

The first of these is how President George Washington stopped a rebellion.

When Congress, in 1791, passed an excise-tax law, levying four pence per gallon on all distilled spirits, the counties west of the Alleghenies rose in violent protest. The Monongahela valley in western Pennsylvania was a good place to grow corn. The Allegheny Mountains separated the area from its markets. The cheapest and easiest way to ship its major products over the hills to market was in the form of distilled liquor. The new whisky excise tax hit hard. In 1794, open rebellion broke out in Pennsylvania. Organized squads of armed infantry began drilling. They declared: "The Whisky Tax will never be collected."

It must have been a sore dilemma for Washington. He was the first leader of a federated nation—a new experiment in modern government. Could the laws that Congress passed be enforced in the member states, even when they were unpopular? Many of those antagonistic mountaineers had been his best soldiers in the Revolution. Yet he did not hesitate. He was President of the United States, sworn to uphold and execute its laws. He called on the governors of four states and ordered fifteen thousand troops to occupy the area, restore order and enforce the law. The rebels quickly put down their arms. Only a handful of them were taken into custody. Only two were tried, convicted and imprisoned, and Washington quickly pardoned them. He could afford to be generous. He had proved what all the world of his time wanted to know: the new federal government could collect the taxes it levied. It could enforce the laws it passed.

THE next important decision I want to cite deals with the manner in which Jefferson expanded the United States into a mighty continental power.

In 1803, the United States purchased from France, for fifteen million dollars, over eight hundred thousand square miles of territory, nearly doubling the size of the Republic.

One of the tests of a great leader is the ability to recognize and seize unexpected opportunity. When President Jefferson sent James Monroe on his historic mission to Napoleon, he was merely concerned with securing freedom for American exporters to ship their goods through the port of New Orleans, then a French possession. Jefferson expected Napoleon to refuse and gave Monroe an ace-in-the-hole—a threat that the United States would make a defensive alliance with Britain, then France's enemy.

To Monroe's surprise, Napoleon was eager to sell the entire French possession of Louisiana. He felt that Britain would probably capture the area anyway. To push the deal, he threw in what we now know as the Louisiana Territory— the entire west side of the Missouri-Mississippi valley, some eight hundred thousand square miles stretching nearly all the way to the Pacific Ocean. At roughly three cents per acre, it was probably history's greatest real estate bargain.

Imagine President Jefferson's excitement when he heard the news! Here was a chance for his struggling little Atlantic seaboard country to become a mighty continental power. But there was a big "if." Jefferson was a strict Constitutionalist. He believed that the survival of the new federal union and the continued freedom of its citizens depended on hewing to the laws of the Constitution right down to the last letter. And nowhere in the Constitution was there any mention of the right to acquire any new territory. What should he do?

Jefferson decided to take a broad general view of his constitutional powers and go ahead with the purchase. He argued that the power to govern territory obviously implies the prior right to acquire it. He relied on our system of checks and balances to stop him if he were wrong. But the Supreme Court upheld his move. Because of Thomas Jefferson's farsighted courage—which included even the courage to modify his own public position—the United States of America was on its way to its historic destiny as a rich, major power.

THE third great decision in our history came when Jackson stopped another rebellion and upheld the power of Congress.

In 1832 the State of South Carolina, under the leadership of United States Vice President John C. Calhoun, called a legislative convention and declared that the federal excise tax law of 1828 was null and void and was therefore no longer enforceable in South Carolina.

In 1828, Congress had passed a tariff law imposing high import duties on textiles, glass, earthenware and paper. The law pleased the industrial North, infuriated the agricultural South. It brought to a head a question that had been debated for many years. Can a state legally nullify the force of an act of Congress within its own borders?

South Carolina, under the leadership of John Calhoun, called a special convention in 1832 and declared that the federal tariff law was nullified in that state. Citizens of South Carolina were ordered to stop paying or collecting it. The state militia was ordered to back them up in their intransigent stand.

Andrew Jackson was President. He was himself a southerner. These were his people, of his own faith, his own kind. What is more, Jackson frankly stated his conviction that the tariff worked injustice to the people of the South. He agreed that it was abominable.

But he denied that nullification was legal. He said it was not even peaceable—that it was an act of open rebellion, directly inciting to treason and war. In a moving speech, he begged the people of South Carolina to honor the Union first and to put states' rights second.

Then, to show that he meant business, he ordered General Winfield Scott to command federal troops in South Carolina, and sent two warships to anchor in Charleston harbor. The tax, President Jackson warned, would be collected by force if necessary. The best way to settled disputes over states' rights, he firmly believed, was by means of debate and compromise—not by threats of rebellion.

THE fourth major decision came when Abraham Lincoln saved the Union.

When Lincoln took the oath of office as President of the

United States on March 4, 1861, the nation was facing one of its darkest hours. Seven states had renounced the Union. Four more would soon join them. Six weeks later, our country's bloodiest conflict started. At a cost of 359,528 northern lives and 133,785 southern lives, peace was finally restored and the Union preserved.

Very few members of my family have shared my admiration for Abraham Lincoln. They were southern in their sympathies. But to me, Lincoln was one of the most effective of our great Presidents when he closed the door for all time on the right of a state to leave the Union. Ironically, the single act for which he is best remembered—the Emancipation Proclamation—is not clearly understood even by those who revere him most.

Lincoln was not an Abolitionist. He believed that slavery was morally wrong. He often expressed his personal wish that all men everywhere could be free. But he believed that under the Constitution it was a matter that each state had the right to decide for itself. He knew very well that the men of the North did not answer his call to arms in order to free the slaves. The objective was to preserve the Union. Everything else was secondary to that goal.

In a letter to Horace Greeley, editor of the New York *Tribune*, Lincoln stated his point of view. It is astonishing that so few people today are familiar with it. He wrote: "If I could save the Union without freeing any slave, I would do it. If I could save it by freeing all the slaves, I would do it. If I could save it by freeing some and leaving others alone, I would also do that."

The Emancipation was conceived as an act of military necessity. Lincoln acted under his emergency wartime powers. Legally speaking, what he did was to seize and dispose of a large amount of private property—something he could never have gotten away with in peacetime, no matter how much he longed to do it.

The Proclamation was a master stroke of psychological warfare. It was intended to underscore the withdrawal of Lee's troops in the Battle of Antietam, an indecisive contest in which the North claimed victory. Lincoln also hoped that it would draw off some of the slave labor forces that were supporting the armies in the South and help swing opinion in Europe, particularly in England, in favor of the North.

Today we have still to solve the problems which the Emancipation has bequeathed us. And if we had had strong, able men in the White House between 1850 and 1860, the issues concerned in the Secession could probably have been settled and the slaves freed peacefully and justly. The Civil War would never have occurred and we would not now be living with its bitter racial aftermath that distorts the harmonious democracy we so wish to show the world.

THE action of Cleveland in saving the two-party system I regard as another turning point in our history.

An aftermath of the Civil War was the almost complete domination of the national political scene by the Republican party, the party of Lincoln and of the victorious North. From 1861 to 1885, the Administration was in Republican hands for six successive terms.

Grover Cleveland, a Democrat, was elected to office in 1884, ending twenty-four years of Republican rule in the

White House. It marked the recovery of our healthy two-party system. It also marked the end of a period in which Congress had pushed chief executives this way and that and usurped many Presidential powers. Cleveland was not the man to stand for that. During his first term, the Presidential vetoes came down like hailstones.

When a President does not have a fight or two with Congress, you know there is something wrong. A man with thin skin has no business being President. These scraps are not personal. It is part of our scheme of government that the executive and legislative branches jealously guard their rights against infringements. But in 1885, Congress had had things pretty much its own way for a long time.

Cleveland vetoed 414 bills during his first Administration. Many of them were private pension bills—thinly disguised graft. He braved the wrath of the Grand Army of the Republic, the politically powerful veteran's organization, when he knocked out the Dependent Pension Bill which would eventually have put nearly every veteran in the United States on the public payroll. He forced through the repeal of the Tenure of Office Act and regained Presidential control over appointment to and removal from executive office.

Under Cleveland, our democracy once again began to function as our founders had intended that it should. Our government was ready to face the massive problems of the twentieth century, prompted by a newly alert public and powered by a Chief Executive who had recovered his independence.

❖   ❖   ❖

A MORE recent event, which has had a profound influence on our life as a nation, took place when Franklin D. Roosevelt helped unite the free world.

Under the Administration of Franklin D. Roosevelt, the United States for the first time committed itself to membership in a world organization of nations. Woodrow Wilson, a generation earlier, was unable to persuade this country to join the League of Nations, but his efforts paved the way for the change in public opinion that eventually resulted in our joining the United Nations.

It took thirty years, two dreadful wars and two great leaders, Wilson and Roosevelt, who literally struggled to their deaths, to lead us to our rightful place in the world.

There are some people who consider Woodrow Wilson's second term a failure because he could not persuade the Senate to let us join the League of Nations. Yet it is quite possible that if Wilson had not tried, Roosevelt could not have succeeded. Both of these men understood what we are dangerously close to forgetting today—that it is the President's duty to lead the nation in the conduct of its foreign affairs. This is a responsibility that cannot be delegated and must not be avoided.

Wilson was a great historian and a great leader. Under him, we became international-minded. He failed only as a politician. He was unable to enlist the support of the "irreconcilables." These senators abused their power to approve treaties, kept us out of the League of Nations and, in my opinion, played a large role in causing World War II.

Roosevelt early recognized the need to keep the United Nations project above and beyond politics. When the United Nations opened for business, Senator Arthur Vandenberg, a

Republican and former isolationist, was a leading member of our delegation. In this way, we showed the world that our isolationist period had come conclusively to an end.

When I became President, my first act was to reaffirm the United States' desire to see a world organization that would preserve peace. Within a few minutes of my taking the oath of office, I announced that we would carry on with the historic assembly, now known as the San Francisco Conference. In this way, at last a mature nation, we joined the world community.

15

Some Thoughts on the Presidency

I DO not think that the people of the United States fully understand the extraordinary character of the office of the President of the United States.

The personalities of some of our Presidents have been so strong that they have eclipsed or obscured the unparalleled nature of the Presidency, diverting attention from that office to themselves.

There are people who would curtail the duties of our Chief Executive because they think that the President has too much power. And there are people who do not trust the President on specific issues, while others want to tie his hands for personal reasons, or for the benefit of certain special groups. What the Presidency needs is a continuing study and a broader understanding of its powers and duties. The use of the broad powers of the office depends upon the knowledge, capacity, experience and personal disposition of the occupant of the White House.

When the founding fathers outlined the Presidency in Article II of the Constitution, they left a great many details vague. I think they relied on the experience of the nation to fill in the outlines. The office of Chief Executive has grown with the progress of our Republic. It has responded to the many demands that our complex society has made upon the government. It has given our nation a means of meeting our greatest emergencies. Today, it is one of the most important factors in our leadership of the free world.

Many diverse elements entered into the creation of the office of the Presidency, springing as it did from the parent idea of the separation of powers. There was the firm conviction of such powerful and shrewd minds as John Adams that the greatest protection against unlimited power lay in an executive secured against the encroachments of a national assembly. Then there were the fears of those who suspected a plot to establish a monarchy on these shores. Others believed that the experience under the Confederation showed, above all, the need for stability through a strong central administration. Finally, there was the need for compromise between these and many other conflicting views.

The result was a compromise—a compromise which that shrewd observer, Alexis de Tocqueville, believed over a hundred and twenty years ago would not work. He thought that the Presidential office was too weak. The President, he thought, was at the mercy of Congress. The President could recommend, to be sure, but he had no power. The power was vested in the Congress. The Congress could disregard his recommendations, overrule his vetoes, reject his nominations. De Tocqueville thought that no man of parts, worthy of leadership, would accept so feeble a role.

This was by no means a foolish view, and there was much in our early history that tended to bear it out. But there is a power in the course of events which plays its own part. In this case again, Justice Holmes' epigram proved true —a page of history is worth a volume of logic. And as the pages of history were written, they unfolded powers in the Presidency not explicitly found in Article II of the Constitution.

In the first place, the President became the leader of a political party. The party under his leadership had to be dominant enough to put him in office, and while often many members regretted it afterward, the majority of the party wanted to do it again. This political party leadership was the last thing the Constitution-makers had contemplated. The President's election was not intended to be mixed up in the hurley-burley of partisan politics. The people were to choose wise and respected men who would meet in calm seclusion and choose a President. The runner-up would be Vice President.

All of this went by the board—though most of the original language remains in the Constitution. Out of the struggle and tumult of the political arena, a new and different President emerged—a man who leads a political party to victory and retains in his hands the power of party leadership. That is, he retains it if he can wrest it, like the sword Excalibur, from the block and wield it.

ANOTHER development in the evolution of the Presidency was connected with the first. As the President came to be elected by the whole people, he became responsible to the whole people. Our people looked to him for leadership and not for passive submission to the rigid limits of a written document. Every hope and every fear of his fellow citizens, almost every aspect of their welfare and activity, falls within the scope of his concern—indeed, within the scope of his duty. Only a man who has held that office can really appreciate that. It is the President's responsibility to look at all questions from the point of view of the whole people. His written and spoken word can command national, often international, attention—again, if he has within him the power to attract and hold that attention.

These powers, which are not explicitly written into the Constitution, are powers which no President can pass on to his successor. They go only to the man who can take and use them. It is these powers, however, quite as much as those enumerated in Article II, which make the Presidential system unique and which give the papers of Presidents their peculiar and revealing importance.

It is through the use of these powers that leadership arises, events are molded and administrations take on their character. Their use can make a Jefferson or a Lincoln Administration; their non-use can make a Buchanan or a Grant Administration.

A study of these aspects of our governmental and political history will save us from self-righteousness—from taking a holier-than-thou attitude toward other nations. For, brilliant and enduring as was the work of our Constitution-makers, they did not devise a foolproof system to protect us against the disaster of weak government—that is, government unable to face and resolve, one way or another, our pressing national problems. Indeed, in some respects, the separation of powers requires stronger executive leadership than does the parliamentary and cabinet system.

Justice Brandeis used to remark that the separation of powers was not devised to promote efficiency in government. In fact, it was devised to prevent one form of efficiency—absolutism or dictatorship. By making the Congress separate and independent in the exercise of its powers, a certain amount of conflict was built into the Constitution. The price of independence is eternal vigilance—plus a good deal of struggle. And this is not a bad thing; on the contrary, it is a good thing for the preservation of the liberty of the people —as long as it does not become conflict for its own sake.

HAVING served in two branches of government, legislative and executive, I think I am expressing a considered and impartial opinion in saying that the powers of the President are much more difficult to exercise and to preserve from encroachment than those of the Congress. In part, this difficulty stems from the problems of our time and from the fact that upon the President falls the responsibility of obtaining action, timely and adequate to meet the nation's needs. Whatever the Constitution says, it is the President who is held responsible for disaster.

And so a successful administration is one of strong Presidential leadership. Weak leadership—or no leadership—produces failure, often chaos and something else. It produces a period of government very similar to that of countries which we think of as being different from ourselves. These are countries where governments are continually falling—where no problem can be decided because the legislature will not support any government which proposes to face problems of real difficulty, where any decision will be unpopular.

This chaos does not result from any inherent weakness of the people of the nation. It is inherent in government where there is no executive strong and stable enough to rally the people to a sustained effort of will and prepared to use its power of party control to the full.

Today, also, one of the great responsibilities and opportunities of the President is to lead and inspire public opinion. The words of a President carry great weight. His acts carry even more. The office of the Presidency is the one organ of our government to which all the people turn when they are beset by fears.

I LIKE to think of eight great men who, in my opinion, were strong Presidents. They were George Washington, Thomas Jefferson, Andrew Jackson, Abraham Lincoln, Grover Cleveland, Theodore Roosevelt, Woodrow Wilson and Franklin D. Roosevelt. One day soon, I hope to write about each of those Presidents, the conditions with which they were faced and the decisions they made to meet them.

We know that some of our Presidents were unwilling to exercise their powers and were sticklers for wordy interpretations of the Constitution. I place Martin Van Buren, Zachary Taylor, Millard Fillmore, Franklin Pierce, James Buchanan and Benjamin Harrison in this class. One or two other Presidents might be added to this list, but their admin-istrations are still being analyzed. To get a more accurate perspective on them, we need more information and more time.

I assume everyone knows that I have always belonged to the Democratic party. One of the deciding reasons for my remaining a Democrat, after intensive study of the history of the United States, was that the Democratic party, in the last decades of the nineteenth century and the first half of the twentieth, had always supported strong Presidents, while the Republican party had been constantly suspicious of strong Presidents, even one of its own (Teddy Roosevelt), and timid about supporting Presidential powers and duties.

The efforts in the past to hamper and restrict the office of the Presidency fall largely into two categories—attempts to contract the inherent powers of the President and at-tempts to cause him to lose prestige.

At the top of the list of endeavors to handicap the Presi-dency is the Twenty-second Amendment to the Constitution. This amendment limits the number of terms a President may hold to two. It also limits the Vice President who succeeds to an unfinished term of a President to one full term, if the one to which he succeeds runs longer than two years. Be-cause it restricts the Presidency and thwarts the right of the people to choose any President they desire, this amendment is a monstrosity—one of the worst ever added to the Con-stitution. It is as bad as that short-lived Prohibition amend-ment. In the event the nation is confronted by a grave emergency, it could be tragic.

The Twenty-second Amendment was passed in 1947 by

the Eightieth Congress and was ratified by the thirty-sixth state, Nevada, in 1951. This amendment was sponsored by that famous Eightieth Congress as a reflection upon a great President, Franklin D. Roosevelt. The moving argument for the passage of the amendment was that it would prevent a President from becoming a dictator. That was just plain nonsense to cover up a bit of political skulduggery. None of our Presidents, regardless of the times or the circumstances, has ever remotely entertained the notion of dictatorship. Of course, if some future President should turn out to have the views of a Hitler or Mussolini, he could grab absolute power, in any term, by taking command of the armed forces and tearing up the Constitution. This is totally unthinkable in the United States. It is the historic background of our ideals and institutions that will prevent dictatorship, not the Twenty-second Amendment.

Another terrible example of a legislative effort to tie the President's hands is the so-called Bricker Amendment. This proposed Constitutional provision would effectively prevent the President from making treaties and executive agreements with foreign governments. It is a real example of living and thinking in terms of the eighteenth century instead of the twentieth. If the Democrats had not rallied to defeat this proposal to handcuff the President in his dealings with foreign governments, this government would have been placed in a sorrowful position in the conduct of our relations with the rest of the world.

Such attempts on the powers of the Presidency are made all the time. Recently, powerful selfish interests tried to cut down the President's power to make international trade agreements. I am sorry to say that some members of my party joined in this escapade.

Another proposal, while it does not seem to be aimed directly at the President, nevertheless is a vicious and subtle assault on his powers. That is the plan, backed by many big businessmen, to place a limit on income tax assessments of twenty-five per cent by Constitutional amendment. This proposed amendment would leave the President and the federal government without the finances to defend the country or to pay its accumulated debts. The result of this kind of reasoning would saddle the cost of the government on those least able to pay.

Some plans that look plausible on the face would also tend to constrict the Presidency by indirection. The proposal to establish a national Presidential primary is in this class. The supporters of the plan do not realize its implications and consequences. Both major parties nominate their Presidential candidates in conventions. This may not be a perfect system but it has produced some of our greatest leaders. The strongest incentive the delegates to these great political conventions have is that they want a man with the best chance to win, and they realize that if they nominate anyone short of that, the country, as a rule, will not take him.

A national Presidential primary would force a candidate to raise a huge sum of money in order to tour the country and make his good points known. No poor man or even one fairly well fixed could finance a national campaign. The money would have to be raised and contributed by the wealthy and the special interests. The nominee would become obligated to contributors, and that would not be good for the country. The President should not be faced with any obligations to special interests, powerful groups or wealthy individuals.

As I write these notes, I am in my office in the Truman Library in Independence. In the bookshelves on one wall are about five hundred volumes of the papers, memoirs and biographies of Presidents of the United States. On the opposite wall are biographies of the great men of history. Most of these books have been read and studied, and I keep adding to them. Obtaining knowledge of the Presidency, the Congress and the rulers of the great countries of the world is a fascinating pursuit. This Truman Library will soon begin to offer scholarships for the study of the Presidency. I hope that scholarships will be offered eventually for the study of the great men of the Congress and the courts of the United States. In short, when all of us know more about the Presidency and the government in general—local, state and national—and begin to appreciate the importance of the President's duties and powers, we will be more zealous about protecting them in every way.

Of course, I do not think that the office of President is perfect as it stands. An erosion of its influence can take place by custom as well as by law or amendment. For one thing, I do not like this present trend toward a huge White House staff.

The President must make his own decisions. He cannot pass the buck up or down. Therefore, he must keep in close touch with the men who run the government at his direction. A layer of Presidential aides has been placed between the President and his appointed officials. Mostly, these aides get in one another's way. They tend to insulate the President. The President needs breathing space. The smaller the staff around him, the better. Information is what he needs. When he has the right information, he is in a position to make the right decisions—and he, and only he, must make them.

There has been a lot of talk lately about the burdens of the Presidency. Decisions that the President has to make often affect the lives of tens of millions of people around the world, but that does not mean that they should take longer to make. Some men can make decisions and some cannot. Some men fret and delay under criticism. I used to have a saying that applies here, and I note that some people have picked it up: "If you can't stand the heat, get out of the kitchen."

16

Battle of the Generals

I WAS more than casually curious to see what the generals would have to say in their recent books on the incidents and conduct of World War II. Since I have had some direct connection with many of those events, I had a fair idea of the strategy and the personalities involved, and I had my own opinion of the claims and counter-claims advanced by some of the more articulate generals.

Now more than ever, I wish that General Marshall had listened to me when I urged him to write his memoirs. Since he was in every sense the chief architect of the grand strategy of the war for the Allies—in Europe and in the Pacific—Marshall's own analysis, I believe, would have been a more balanced report on what was intended and what actually took place.

I think it would have been a more objective study than many of the books by military men that have been published since the war—certainly more so than some I have read recently.

I must admit that I have found them all interesting

reading and I think they serve a useful purpose. We all know mistakes were made, and in looking back it is always easier to recognize them. Mistakes have been made in every war.

It is normal after wars to find some generals arguing in public about the blunders that might have been avoided, and how their ideas of strategy might have resulted in earlier victory. Many books, written by generals since time began, seem to me to be mainly alibis. But the recent crop of military memoirs tend to be a little more personal and vindictive.

I find that personal rivalries and disappointments impel the authors to color what happened, and thus often distort the true picture. Very few soldiers have written about their campaigns with the uncomplicated simplicity and directness of Caesar in his *Commentaries*.

Alexander the Great, George Washington and Robert E. Lee, among the great military leaders of the past, never wrote about their feats on the battlefield. When Napoleon attempted to write his memoirs while at St. Helena, the result was inadequate and inaccurate.

George Washington, although he kept a daily diary to keep himself informed, did not write a book about his own deeds, preferring that history make the final judgment. Washington possessed that rare quality of greatness which enabled him to make as distinguished a contribution to statesmanship as he did to military leadership. No other American to this day approaches him in ability to combine the two qualities.

General Ulysses S. Grant, whose feats were decisive in bringing about the end of the War Between the States but who was a disappointment as President, did write his memoirs, but they proved full of inaccuracies.

Statesmen and heads of government during wars have not and could not escape criticism for their versions of what happened when they were in charge. Woodrow Wilson, a great President, war leader and historian, would not write a book about Versailles, preferring to leave the final appraisal to history. I wish that President Wilson had written his own version of what occurred there.

Unfortunately, history is too often a combination of official records and source material, with an interpretation by some historian of what he presumes to have been in the minds of the people he writes about. Many modern historians, I find, rely too much on published contemporary history, with inadequate knowledge of or even research into the accuracy of such published material. In many respects, they are like Plutarch, who, although lacking the ease of picking up printed gossip, often included oral gossip and legends as actual facts. I think our children today have passed on to them too much that is fiction and nonsense that is accepted as true history.

The astonishing degree of inaccuracy of facts and events and the deliberate distortions of intentions, particularly in recent times, have often disturbed me as I read the newspapers and magazines and listen to radio reports. Until I became President, I could not fully assess the extent of the inaccuracies and distortions to which the public was exposed and upon which historians often base their conclusions and interpretations. When, as President, I saw the damaging effect that inaccuracies and false reports had on the people, I decided that I would leave a written record based on my first-hand knowledge of what I did and what I had in mind to do. I am certain no one could know better what was in my mind than I did.

The speculation and assumptions, for example, about my feelings on the use of the atomic bomb on Nagasaki and Hiroshima were as contradictory as the varying stories written on the subject, and most of them had no foundation in fact.

Throughout my political life, I had, of course, kept written notes from time to time on what was going on and what I did about it. This was a sort of loose diary, and sometimes I wish that I had been of a nature to keep a daily diary.

I often marvel at the details in Washington's diary, which include seemingly trivial points that today shed considerable light on the person and character of our first President. As a matter of fact, Washington's habit of recording the daily weather in so comprehensive a manner led to the establishment of the first weather bureau of the government.

Therefore, while I was yet able and in good health, I did write my memoirs. I set down the principal facts of those eventful years as I knew them, based on careful research of the official documents and my private papers.

I did omit material for reasons of security and out of consideration for certain persons. I have, however, placed this material under seal in the Truman Library to be made available after a suitable number of years, and after the persons concerned and I will have passed on.

In some respects, I think the contending generals of the

last decade might have kept from publication some of their views and thoughts of each other until another time. But I do not think there is any real harm in the current battle of the generals. Regardless of what they say about each other, this kind of feuding is bound to bring out more facts, and maybe even cut some generals down to size. Quarrels between generals who fought on the same side are sometimes as bitter as those between commanders of opposing armies, and they are as old—or older—than the strife between Caesar and Pompey.

In our own history, there was one general who was above attack, and he was Washington. But while Washington escaped the open criticism and jealousy of the military, he was, lest we forget, bitterly assailed and maligned when he was President.

In the War Between the States, the only general who remained in command and above criticism throughout was Robert E. Lee. I am sorry to see that, in recent years, efforts have been made by some historians to reduce the true stature and greatness of Robert E. Lee as a leader and military man. I do not think they are going to succeed. Increasing criticism is also being voiced about Stonewall Jackson these days.

Virtually all generals and admirals in all our wars have been criticized, but the argument is especially heated when one general gets into open controversy with another, as in the differences between Winfield Scott and Zachary Taylor in the Mexican War. And in the Spanish-American War, Admiral Sampson and Admiral Schley got into a bad fuss as to who won the Battle of Santiago.

Recently, General Eisenhower has been the subject of violent criticism by Field Marshal Montgomery and Field Marshal Allenbrook. Of course, we have to remember that with our entry into the Second World War, the United States for the first time was put in complete command of the Allied Forces. I suspect that it was a hard pill for some of the British generals to swallow. They probably had thought there was no military talent in the United States on a level with their own.

They were mistaken. But I have an idea some of them are going to keep talking about it for a long, long time. I do not think it will do any harm to the reputation of those men who really made great contributions to the winning of the war—particularly General Marshall, General Eisenhower and General Bradley.

History will make its assessment of Eisenhower as a soldier and a leader. I expressed my own judgment of him and his military and diplomatic gifts when I appointed him Chief of Staff and recalled him to organize and head up NATO—the North Atlantic Treaty Organization—to safeguard the West.

During the war he coordinated the Allies, kept them together and made the historic crossing of the English Channel to invade Nazi-occupied Europe. I think he came out of the situation in Europe in very good shape, no matter what others may think or say.

But it was General Marshall, in my opinion, who was the "brains." He was the man who really made the military organization work, both in the Atlantic and the Pacific, and this is what brought about victory.

I tried to persuade General Marshall to write his memoirs and set down the facts as he saw them when he was Chief of Staff of the United States, and in reality Chief of Staff of all the Allies. But he refused to do this. General Marshall was of the opinion that, since all the facts would eventually come out, it was not necessary for him to write his own evaluation of what happened. And he was especially concerned not to write anything that would hurt anyone. He said that any criticism he had of anyone he had already expressed, and he had done so at a time when it was essential to correct a situation or take action.

But along toward the last of his life, when attacks were made on him that were motivated politically and contained false allegations, he made up his mind to dictate his own observations for the record. Unfortunately, his health began to fail and he did not live long enough to complete the task. I hope that whatever he did manage to have set down will be made available to the people in some form.

General Omar Bradley, who was in direct command of the largest field army on the western front, was one of our greatest military leaders. And two admirals of the Second World War stand out in my mind. They were Admiral Chester A. Nimitz and Admiral Ernest A. King. I regard Nimitz as the greatest naval strategist and commander of the war in the Pacific. Admiral King was a crusty martinet. I used to have difficulties with him. But he was a great Chief of Naval Operations, and he was responsible for the reorganization of the navy after Pearl Harbor.

I am of the opinion that the top military leaders of our

Allies were outstanding men and played significant roles in the over-all victory. The important thing is that the war was won.

There is no harm when generals have their controversies after the fighting is over, when their differences cannot damage or hamper the conduct of war. The trouble throughout history has been that generals tend to engage in personal quarrels and become diverted from the main task of defeating the enemy.

17

No Monuments
to the Living

IF the Truman Library in Independence had been conceived as a memorial to me personally, I would have
done everything I could to prevent its establishment during
my lifetime.

For one thing, I do not believe that monuments any
more than memorials should be erected to a living person.
And where a person has been entrusted with high office of
public trust, I think it only fair, not to say prudent, to wait
until his life has been completed before we decide whether
or not to put up a monument to him.

I encouraged the building of the Library only because
it was to be a center for the study of all the Presidents and
the Presidency as well as the history of the United States.
And I wanted the building located in the Midwest so that it
would be of easy access to many hundreds of educational
institutions that, in this part of the United States, do not
have the same opportunity for research in original material

that eastern schools and colleges have available to them.

To a certain extent, I wanted to follow the examples of two former Presidents, Franklin D. Roosevelt and Herbert Hoover, who wisely saw the need for housing their personal and private papers so that they might be preserved and made available to scholars, teachers and historians. I had a large collection of papers and documents which I had accumulated during my years in the White House and which needed to be kept together and stored somewhere. Because all of my papers were to be kept there, I agreed to the designation of the building as the Truman Library.

When a President leaves the White House at the completion of his tenure of office, he takes all his papers with him. By historical precedent, beginning with George Washington, the files of a President have always been considered his personal property.

The papers of Presidents are among the most valuable source material of our history. They are the records, and in many cases the only surviving records, of an administration, except for executive orders, messages to Congress and formal statements. And recently, Presidential press conferences have also come to be considered part of the President's record.

It may come as a surprise to many that although there is in *The Congressional Record* an official account of everything that is said and done in the Congress, there is no similar official publication of even the President's public statements. Students have to search newspaper files and other sources to find out what former Presidents have said before the year of 1957. The bulk of the history of any administration is to be found in the files of the President's

Fritz Henle

This is one of my favorite photographs.
It was taken in December, 1959.

My father, John Truman, at the age of 30. Dad grew up in Jackson County, Missouri, but spent most of his life on a farm outside Independence. He taught me the virtue of hard work—by personal example.

Martha (Ellen Young) Truman, my mother. She met my father as neighbors usually met in the farm areas in those days and they were married on December 28, 1881. My mother taught me that all people are basically good, and that is one lesson I never had to unlearn. Neither this picture nor the one of my father has ever been published before. These pictures were taken in Kansas City in 1881.

An excellent picture of my mother at the age of eighty. She was always looking at the good things in life and taught her children to appreciate them.

One of my favorite portraits of Mrs. Truman and myself. We evidently enjoyed this affair.

Mrs. Truman and I pose on the front porch of 219 Delaware Street in Independence, where we have lived for many years. The house is over a hundred years old and is still as pleasant and comfortable as when it was built.

My early-morning walk takes me through the deserted "main street" of Independence. I didn't know the sign was there, but it is good advice.

My brother Vivian (sitting on the bench next to me) and I talk over affairs at our family farm outside Grandview. We usually meet every Sunday and discuss business and family affairs.

Bradley Smith from Rapho-Guillumette

Back home now, I run on the same schedule I've followed for years—up at 5:30, dress, then downstairs to get the paper the boy has flipped over the fence. In summer, I settle down on the back porch for an hour, reading the news and my correspondence. Some folks are surprised when they see me putting my nickel in the parking meter like any other private citizen, or when I show up for lunch at a popular cafeteria in Independence.

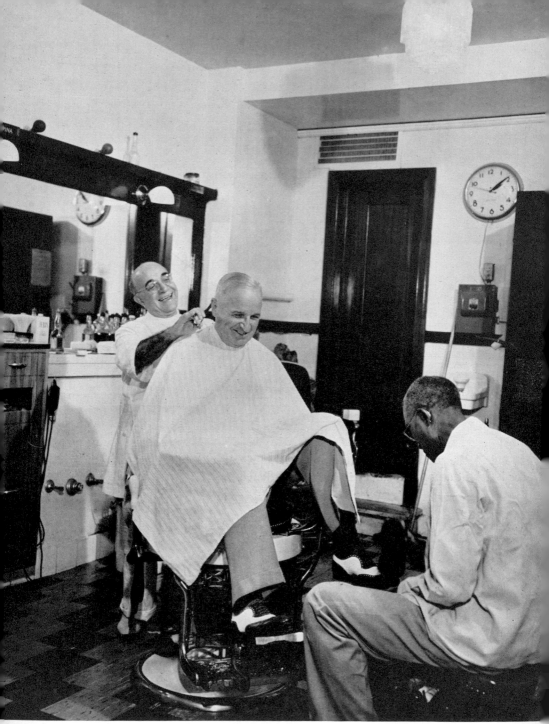

One of my favorite places at home is the 10th Street barbershop. After many years' experience, Frank Spina knows just how I like my hair cut. Frank was in Battery D, 129th Field Artillery, 35th Division. I was his Captain. Bob, the porter, is the best in town.

Bradley Smith from Rapho-Guillumette

Often when I come home in the afternoon, I find Bess playing bridge with her friends. Since they don't welcome my kibitzing, I usually go upstairs and take a nap. Below, my secretary, Miss Rose Conway and I at work in my office in the Truman Library.

Bradley Smith from Rapho-Guillumette

Mrs. Truman and I spend most of our evenings reading. She likes entertainment in her reading while I usually prefer history books, biographies and an occasional whodunit. We have spent many pleasant evenings in this room.

The Truman family at a banquet in our honor shortly after we arrived home in Independence.

N. Y. Daily News Photo

I cut a cake on my seventieth birthday at the Waldorf Astoria in New York, as Mrs. Truman, Margaret and Mayor Robert F. Wagner of New York look on.

Brown Brothers

I have a special visitor at the Library. He is Jerry Hammond, a muscular dystrophy patient, who has a cheery smile for me despite his affliction.

Harry S. Truman Library Photograph by Harry Barth, Independence, Missouri

A wonderful occasion, with Margaret and Clifton Daniel, Jr.,
leaving the church after their wedding. It was a lovely affair
at home in Independence.

Jack Benny comes to Kansas City to help us raise over fifty thousand dollars for the Kansas City Symphony Orchestra. Benny kept the orchestra in stitches, and I joined in the fun. Jack later played a return engagement for the benefit of the Truman Library. I had a good time showing him around.

Our grandchildren come to visit us in Independence to spend their first Christmas at our home. Mrs. Truman and I greet Margaret and her children at the railroad station. The young man in my arms is Clifton Truman Daniel. Coming up behind Mrs. Truman is the nurse, Miss Nutzman, holding William Wallace Daniel, then seven months old. In the Truman Library, below, Clifton Truman Daniel shows an early independence, negotiating the stairway on his own. I'm trying to keep in step with him.

Clifton Truman Daniel hunting for more information at the
Truman Library. He liked shiny things, and especially liked to
get his hands on them.

office, in his correspondence, his notes, the personal letters he writes and the personal letters he receives.

It is my opinion that the only accurate source of information on which to make a proper historical assessment of the performances of past Presidents is in the Presidential files. This is why I think these documents not only ought to be preserved but should be placed and arranged so that they can be used.

Too many Presidential papers in the past have been widely scattered and, in some instances, destroyed and lost. The federal government is now trying to acquire and assemble, either through purchase or through gifts, substantial collections of Presidential papers that were gathered by former Presidents but not kept intact by the Presidents' descendants.

Today there are important collections of papers of most of the thirty-two Presidents but few of them are complete. Twenty-three of the Presidential collections are in the Library of Congress but seven of them are fragmentary. For the most part they have not been indexed and so they can be utilized only by highly specialized students. For this reason, I wanted to make sure that my papers would be kept complete as public papers and available for study.

I have felt so strongly about the need for making the Presidential papers in the Library of Congress available for general study that on June 21, 1957, I went to Washington to testify before a Congressional committee. I spoke in support of a bill introduced by Congressman John McCormack of Massachusetts, Democratic Majority Leader of the House, which provided funds for the indexing of these collections and for their preservation and distribution to other libraries through microfilming. Congress approved this bill, and these papers are now being indexed.

The volume of Presidential papers in recent times has grown to huge proportions. In my case over a half million documents and papers were accumulated in a year—more than 3,500,000 altogether—and I felt a library to house them was a necessity. But I wanted to establish in Independence facilities for the study not only of my own papers, but also the papers of all of the Presidents. Initially, this can be accomplished in part through loans from other libraries, and eventually I hope to have a complete set of all Presidential papers by microfilm.

In this way, students interested in the study of the Presidency and the history of the United States will not have to travel from place to place in search of information. We hope to have it for them in Independence.

In addition, the Truman Library will house the personal papers not only of members of my Cabinet, but other historic documents. For example, I have discussed with the archivist of the Vatican the microfilming of some interesting papers in connection with American history that we ought to have here, and I have been assured of full cooperation. I envisage the possibility of cooperation with other great world centers where papers are stored dealing with early phases of American history.

Some of my hopes that the Library would be a center for students and scholars have been realized. In the first years of the Library's existence, more than three hundred thousand visitors have passed through, and I have talked with many students who assembled in the auditorium to listen to brief impromptu lectures followed by question and answer sessions. I talk to four or five groups a day when I am at home.

I have hopes that we will establish scholarships for needy students to enable them to study at the Library. The archivist in charge, Dr. Philip C. Brooks, director, assisted by a group of professional archivists, has done a wonderful job in organizing the papers and exhibits. The papers that have been opened to the students include about three-fourths of the two principal segments of my White House central files, files of some members of my immediate staff, and a portion of the papers representing my services as a senator.

The Library is now part of the archives of the United States which maintains and operates it. It was presented as a gift to the government after it had been built by funds subscribed privately by people of all walks of life and of all faiths and political parties. The people who have contributed to the funds to make this Library possible have my eternal gratitude. Nothing that has happened to me during or since the Presidency has given me such deep and abiding satisfaction.

I turned over to the government all of my papers and the gifts that were sent to me from all parts of the world when I was President. The gifts are now on public exhibit. On February 12, 1957, in offering my papers to the federal government, I said:

"It is my purpose to make my papers available for study and research as soon as possible and to the fullest extent possible. However, since the President of the United States is the recipient of many confidences from others, and since the inviolability of such confidences is essential, it will be necessary to withhold from public scrutiny certain papers and classes of papers for varying periods."

The formal transfer of the Library took place on the day of dedication on July 6, 1957. It was a great honor and privilege for me to welcome not only my neighbors and friends but prominent men and women from government, politics, education, churches, labor, industry and agriculture, who came long distances to take part in the dedication ceremonies. Their names are forever enshrined in my memory.

There were many wonderful addresses, and I would like to quote here a passage from the main dedication speech delivered by the Chief Justice of the United States, the Honorable Earl Warren. He said:

"This is an important event in the life of the nation and I am happy to participate in it. The Library which we dedicate is destined to become a midwestern center of study and research, not only for the period of Mr. Truman's Presidency, but also for the whole complex picture of events surrounding it.

"The impetus it provides for extending the research resources of this great section, which has meant so much to the development of the nation as a whole, represents a milestone in American history."

18

Spot Decisions

THE most dangerous course a President can follow in a time of crisis is to defer making decisions until they are forced on him and thereupon become inevitable decisions. Events then get out of hand and take control of the President, and he is compelled to overcome situations which he should have prevented. When a President finds himself in that position, he is no longer a leader but an improviser who is driven to action out of expediency or weakness.

In normal times, lack of Presidential leadership may be harmless, though it can hardly be considered a national asset. But in times of crisis, irresoluteness on the part of a President can do the nation great harm. It can, in fact, damage a situation beyond anyone's ability to overcome it later. I have often thought that if the three Presidents preceding Lincoln—Buchanan, Pierce and Fillmore—had acted as they should have, it is more than likely that the War Between the States might have been averted.

Not only must a President be fully informed but he must be constantly alert to what lies ahead. And he can see

261

ahead only if he has a sense of history and understands the times he lives in.

If a President is so equipped and so endowed, he can make decisions almost instinctively. Sometimes these decisions are instantaneous, and they may be interpreted by some persons as snap judgments. But actually they are rooted in a man's capacity to see clearly what lies ahead and the ability to act quickly. Otherwise the affairs a President has to tackle will crowd in on him and swamp him.

All the time I was President, one event followed another with such rapidity that I was never able to afford the time for prolonged contemplation. I had to make sure of the facts. I had to consult people. But to have hesitated when it was necessary to act might well have meant disaster in many instances.

Many of the important decisions I had to make in the White House were what I described to myself as "spot decisions." By "spot decisions," I meant decisions which were almost instinctive with me—when I had to confront an emergency or serious situation.

I never revealed to anyone what my "spot decision" was in advance of calling for all the facts available and consulting the experts or the departments of government involved. Once the facts were examined and the experts heard, I then made the final decision. Looking back, I find that my final decisions usually corresponded to my first "spot decisions."

I HAVE been asked whether I have any regrets about any of the major decisions I had to make as President. I have none.

And there were many things that had to be done that might have been handled some other way. But considering the information available at the time and the circumstances prevailing when I had to make many of my decisions, I do not see how I could have acted very differently.

A man can find more time to contemplate a situation after it has come about. Looking at the results, he might wonder why it could not have been handled differently. But whenever I felt a mistake had been made, I always tried to remedy the mistake by making another decision. Everybody makes mistakes and the important thing is to correct them, once they are discovered. Sometimes you have a choice of evils, in which case you try to take the course that is likely to bring the least harm.

I am not one who believes it does any good to cry over past mistakes. You have got to keep looking ahead and going straight ahead all the time, making decisions and correcting the situation as you go along. This calls for a fundamental policy, a basic outlook, for the making of major foreign and domestic decisions. Otherwise the operations of the government would be reduced to improvisation—and inevitable trouble. A President who hesitates or temporizes usually is not certain of what he wants, and he is greatly handicapped when he has to act without a clear-cut policy.

A President ought not to worry whether a decision he knows he has to make will prove to be popular. The question is not whether his actions are going to be popular at the time but whether what he does is right. And if it is right in the long run it will come out all right. The man who keeps his ear to the ground to find out what is popular will be in trouble. I usually say that a man whose heart is in the right place and who is informed is not likely to go very far wrong when he has to act.

Of course, each President has his own way of dealing with matters that confront him. The mental habits of a President are as influential as any of the other factors which impel him to make the kind of decision he makes and the swiftness with which he acts. I found myself constantly absorbed in what was pending, from the time I arose until I went to bed. In bed I would try to read something in history which might help me form an opinion as to the course I had to take.

That is the nature of the Presidency, and it is impossible to detach yourself from constant preoccupation with it. But when I went to sleep, I did not carry my burdens with me, so that I was able to start refreshed in the morning.

A President's performance depends a great deal on the information he has and the information he is able to get. I sought the background of every important question that confronted me. I talked with people interested in the welfare of the country who could give me their viewpoint exactly as they thought and believed, no matter what they thought my own opinion was on a particular subject. And frank opinions were hard to get. Too many people tried to find out what I wanted to hear and then gave it to me. But the people I wanted around me did not do that.

I made it my business as President to listen to people in all walks of life and in all fields of endeavor and experience. I did not see only the people who ought to be seen—that is, those who were "well connected." I always tried to be a good listener. But since the responsibility for making decisions had to be mine, I always reserved judgment.

THE reason that led me to set up the Central Intelligence Agency was to make sure that all the vast amount of information available to the different departments of the government would be coordinated and made immediately available to the President—without being edited or interpreted by any one department.

When a crisis came along, such as the one connected with General MacArthur or the Berlin airlift or the aggression against Korea, I was confronted with making far-reaching decisions. Once I made up my mind, I acted. And I did not worry about the action I took. If you are going to walk the floor and worry yourself to death every time you have to make a decision, or if you fail to make up your mind, then you are not suited for the job.

I am frequently asked how much a President depends upon advice and directions from his Cabinet or staff or military leaders or advisers. I always point out that it is absolutely essential for a President to have information and advice. But he does not take directions, because it is the President's responsibility alone to give directions.

One of the things that intrigued me in reading history has been to find out how the great leaders of the world reached decisions. As I look at some of the great decisions of the past, I am inclined to believe that the leaders who made them possessed an almost intuitive sense of the future. Their greatness lay in the fact that they could see further ahead than any of the others around them—further than any of their contemporaries.

I think much of the greatness of our nation has been achieved as a result of the leaders we have had. The wisdom of the framers of the Constitution is apparent, I think, in their vision of the future. And every one of our Presidents who rose to greatness had the gift of projecting himself into the future.

I am not suggesting, of course, that a man can anticipate with any degree of certainty what the future holds in store for any man or any nation. But the actions of a wise leader can and often do have a profound influence on the future.

19

The Atom and War

I HOPE the world will not soon forget the terrible slaughter of human beings that went on in the six years of the Second World War. I hope we will remember that the anguish and ravages visited upon civilian populations were caused almost entirely by weapons that were regarded as "conventional."

I abhor war and I am opposed to any kind of killing—whether by atomic bomb or bow and arrow. War is killing on a mass scale and it is war that we must eliminate—or it will eliminate us.

Yet in this year of 1960 we are engaged in a weapons race, the most dangerous weapons race in all history. There is nothing more urgent confronting the people of all nations than the banning of all nuclear weapons under a foolproof system of international control. And general disarmament cannot come too soon if we are to direct our energies and our resources towards the improvement of the lot of man.

But the biggest mistake we could make would be to delude ourselves into believing that the danger of war would

267

be eliminated if we merely abolished nuclear weapons and reduced other armaments.

Let us not become so preoccupied with weapons that we lose sight of the fact that war itself is the real villain and the scourge of mankind. And it is war—and the causes that lead to war—that must be abolished.

Any weapon that kills—large or small—is evil when in the hands of a killer. Through the long centuries of the history of man, the weapons of war have grown increasingly destructive, but instead of discouraging war, the fact is that wars have increased in frequency and in scale.

There is little hope for the future of the world unless we put an end to wars—now that the world has the potential means of total destruction. This should give us an opportunity to get to the heart of the problem—the abolition of war.

IT was my fate to make the decision to use the first atomic bomb to bring about the end of a terrible war.

When President Roosevelt authorized the vast undertaking to develop an atomic bomb, he had but one purpose —to hasten the winning of a war that had been forced on us. We were in a frenzied race with Nazi Germany to be the first to produce an atomic weapon. At that time the Germans were believed to be ahead of us. We knew that if Hitler were the first to succeed, we and our allies would find ourselves in a hopeless position.

Realizing the gravity of the situation, President Roosevelt wasted no time and spared no effort and resources to make certain that we prevailed against the ruthless men in the Pacific as well as in Europe.

Roosevelt was able to call on some of the world's foremost scientists and had at his side that great American, Henry L. Stimson, to help guide and see the project through its many difficult stages. Secretary Stimson in his diary has recorded the true objective that motivated this nation in developing an atomic weapon.

Soon after I succeeded to the Presidency, upon the death of President Roosevelt, I was informed of the atomic developments about which I was totally unaware, so carefully had the secret been guarded for three years. I called in a committee of authorities in science, education and government for their opinions and advice on the use of the atomic bomb if it became necessary. I asked the chiefs of staff for their judgment and estimate of how long the Japanese could hold out and how many lives—American and Japanese—it would cost to invade the main island of Japan.

Earlier I had already authorized the chiefs of staff to move over a million American troops for a final attack on Japan. Many American units were assembled at the jumping-off places in the Pacific, and many were en route to the Pacific area from the United States and from Europe to prepare for the invasion.

At Potsdam, Stalin had informed me that it would take three months before Russia could be ready to open a second front against Japan. And during the Potsdam conference I consulted with Prime Minister Churchill on the use of the bomb against Japan, since the United States had shared the development of the bomb with Great Britain. Churchill and his military leaders were for using the bomb.

On July 28, Prime Minister Suzuki declared that Japan would ignore the Potsdam declaration of July 26. In that declaration we had offered Japan the choice between surrender with hope for an honorable future, and "inevitable and complete destruction."

The Japanese warlords were making a fanatical stand. And a million and a half Japanese troops were on the Chinese mainland available for the defense of Japan proper.

It was my responsibility as President to force the Japanese warlords to come to terms as quickly as possible with the minimum loss of lives.

I then made my final decision. And that final decision was mine alone to make.

Almost immediately after the dropping of the second atomic bomb, the Japanese surrendered. The most horrible war in all history, with its casualties mounting to over thirty million, was thus brought to an end.

THE big obstacle to peace today is the fact that the Communist rulers of Russia and China have been so concerned with keeping themselves in power and seeking to dominate the world. They have little concern with the peace of the world or even the survival of their own people.

The Russian people at no time had any reason to fear aggression from the free world. I can state unequivocally that the people and government of the United States have never had any ulterior designs against the Russian people or their land. As a matter of fact, three Presidents of the United States made four long journeys to meet with Russian leaders, at places of their own convenience, in an effort to get Russia to cooperate in the interests of world peace.

I would remind some of our neutralist friends, and those who are so easily impressed by Russian propaganda and so critical of their true friends in the West, of a very important fact: soon after the establishment of the United Nations, the United States made the most challenging offer in history to bring about reduction and control of armaments.

We were the sole possessors of the atomic bomb. Yet we sponsored and we were prepared to enter into an agreement to place the control of atomic weapons in the United Nations under a system of international inspection.

But Russia—having no atomic bomb, yet loudly professing her peaceful intentions—wrecked this plan.

Obviously, Russia did not want any disarmament or arms control, except under terms that would leave her free to do as she wished. With the war at an end, Stalin and Molotov were once again busy subverting governments. They never fooled me after Potsdam.

Cynically using the United Nations as a propaganda platform Stalin and Molotov sought to divert attention from their subversive moves by falsely attributing the world's growing tensions and anxieties to our possession of the atomic bomb.

By refusing to agree to a system of international inspection and control of armaments, the Kremlin paved the way for the atomic and nuclear weapons and missile race. They thus destroyed the hope of mankind to take a first important and realistic step toward removing the threat of nuclear warfare with its unimaginable horrors.

For this, Soviet Russia will have to make full accounting before history.

But this is no time for despair. On the contrary, Soviet behavior points the way to our future conduct when faced with similar historical situations. What we must do is to combine resoluteness with patience.

WE must maintain our strength and bide our time. Let us not give the impression that we will hesitate to act if provoked, and let us avoid the dangerous business of weakening our military strength, lest we encourage the Kremlin to bolder adventures. I have had many opportunities to size up the methods of the Kremlin leaders, not only face to face but also in the light of historic perspective.

I have great faith in people, whatever their race or wherever they are. They value freedom above all else, and no conqueror or dictator can ever hold them down for long.

I think that in our lifetime we may hope to see a significant change take place in Russia. But we must act with wisdom and strength in the light of history. We may even hasten that day—if the Russian people can be given to understand that their leaders are misleading them and that their leaders will not be allowed to embark on a new imperialism. Together with our friends and Allies in the free world, we can prevent a tragedy of an overexpanded Russia. The real danger confronting free men today stems not alone from Communist imperialistic militarism but from its insidious perversion of men's minds.

Yet, I do not believe that Soviet Russia can long attract

and hold masses of people to her way of life any place where the individual is not subordinate to the state. In four decades since the Communists took over Russia, not a single nation has voluntarily adopted Communism in a free election.

Russia will not be stopped in her over-all design of conquest to force slavery upon free peoples in the guise of liberation—by soft words and smiling countenances, and, least of all, by panicky reaction to Russia's propaganda moves. We must not at any time falter in maintaining our strong position, no matter what it costs, since we are the principal discouraging force to Communist imperialism—and to war.

This is no policy of despair; it is the course of prudence and hope. Time is on the side of the free peoples of the world, and until the Russian and Chinese people are free to assume their responsibility in helping to guard the peace of the world, we must do everything we can to discourage Russian dictators from embarking on mad ventures that will eventually lead to World War III.

I Write What I Think

NOTE: The material that follows has been especially selected to record in book form my thoughts and observations during certain periods of crisis in recent years. It is my belief that these comments are applicable to many serious problems facing the world today.

—HARRY S. TRUMAN

I LIKE to write. But writing does not always come easy to me. I attach more importance to what I have to say than how I say it. Yet I have to weigh carefully what I put into words because of the office I once held.

I like to use the simplest words I can. The simplest words make for the best communication. Much of the Bible —the King James version—is an example of what I mean, and so is Shakespeare.

When I was approached by several newspaper syndicates to write a regular commentary on important news developments, I declined—at first. Up to 1957 I had made my comments on the news in press interviews and speeches.

But as world tensions mounted, and the pressure on me for frequent comment increased from all parts of the world, I thought it best to express my opinions in written form— carefully thought out—so that I could be constructively helpful in anything I had to say.

I hoped that in this way I could help throw some additional light on events related to world problems with which I had to deal as President.

I intended to be completely forthright, and objective, in my comments. I would be critical if the facts warranted but not in a partisan political sense.

Bipartisanship is essential to the successful conduct of foreign policy by the President of the United States, and to the extent that I thought the President was expressing the basic American foreign policy, I would give him my support.

Thus, four years after I ceased having personal responsibility for the conduct of foreign affairs, I undertook to write for the North American Newspaper Alliance.

My first article was published January 13, 1957.

I have here included what I had to say in some of the articles about the problems that still confront us in a world trying to avert another catastrophe.

The challenge of Khrushchev and the Russian missiles, the search for nuclear control and disarmament, the threat of Red China, the turmoil in the Middle East, the Berlin crisis in Germany, the continuation of the Cold War and the junkets of personal diplomacy—all these are still dominating the affairs of the world. And it is about these things that I comment in this section.

I publicly supported the President when in January, 1957, he asked for special powers from the Congress to deal with the emergency in the Middle East.

This is the position I took:

If I were now a member of the United States Senate, I would support the request of the President for congressional authorization to use the armed forces of the United States against any Communist or Communist-dominated aggressor in the Middle East. And I would quickly approve granting him the funds he seeks to extend economic aid to help the Middle East nations maintain their independence.

Congress has no alternative but to go along with the

President in this program to prevent the Russians from taking over the whole strategic Middle East, so vital to the economy and peace of the world. The situation is too dangerous to delay action on these requests for any partisan or political considerations. The President, who in this emergency should speak for all of us and have the full backing of Congress and the people, must act decisively.

I have felt all along that the steps the President now proposes should have been taken when the Russians began to move into the Middle East by shipments of arms and technicians to Egypt. But I hope that with courageous and wise handling of our future foreign policy, there is yet time to avert the folly and tragedy of another world war. I have had to deal with the Russians in a succession of crises when, within three days after I became President, I had to tell Russian Foreign Minister Molotov at the White House that peace was a two-way street and that we would expect Russia to live up to her agreements. From that time on, from Potsdam, Iran, Berlin, Greece and Turkey to Korea and to my last days in the White House, I found that only plain speaking and forceful action held any hope of checking the Russians from plunging us all into war.

Now that the President proposes to adopt a clear-cut policy of action, we should do everything to back him up. We must at this stage accept the President's assessment of what the situation is, for only the President is in possession of all the facts, and should therefore be in a position to tell us the true state of affairs around the world. It is the President who must exercise his constitutional authority to make foreign policy, and he cannot delegate that authority either to members of his administration, or to Congress, or to the United Nations.

But Congress, too, must do its part to enable the President to carry out his announced policies by voting him adequate funds. At the same time, Congress will, and should, insist on being more fully informed and henceforth more frequently consulted.

The United Nations was established largely through the initiative and support of the United States and has its home here. It is growing in influence and power as a force for peace.

But the United Nations was never intended to assume any of the burden of making foreign policy for the United States. To do so would weaken us and wreck the United Nations. For until other free nations grow in strength, the United Nations will continue to draw its strength from its strongest link—the United States. The League of Nations collapsed without us and the United Nations could crumble if we falter and fail in our unique responsibilities to help maintain the peace of the world.

We cannot hesitate, and we dare not falter in what we must do in the Middle East. The peace and economy of the whole world depend upon the resources concentrated in that area. So long as these resources are available to all nations, unhampered by capricious and tyrannical barriers, the chances for peace will be good. We must do all that we can to ensure free access of this area to all nations. But Russian intrigues and designs to move into the Middle East would deny the world the free access it must have to survive and would inevitably lead to war. Let us make no mistake. This is what Russia is after—control of these resources.

The proposals made by the President, when approved by the Congress, will strengthen the position of the free world. But I do not think they go far enough.

I suggest that certain further steps need to be taken to undo the Russian encroachments in the Middle East and check new penetrations there. Recurring armed clashes and flare-ups, arising from ancient and special troubles in this area, must be settled soon, or else Russia will continue to exploit these troubles for her own expansionist purposes.

These are the steps I have in mind:

First: An embargo ought to be imposed on the shipment of all arms and ammunition by Russia to the Middle East. It would be desirable to have an embargo on shipments of all arms to the Middle East by all nations until tensions subside and security pacts and disarmament agreements in the area can be worked out. Arms and ammunition shipped into the area should go only to the Emergency Forces of the United Nations stationed in that area. I hear the Russians are continuing shipment of arms to Syria, and I expect they will resume shipments to Egypt. Russia must be warned that these must stop. When Russia began penetration of the Middle East by sending arms to Egypt more than a year ago we should have warned the Kremlin that we would not stand for this trouble-making maneuver. All we had to do was to say, "You can't do that" and be ready to back it up. All we would have needed to back up this warning was to put a couple of cruisers at the end of the Black Sea Straits and a couple of cruisers and air carriers in the Eastern Mediterranean. Our past experience—as in the case of the Berlin Airlift—showed that the Russians would not dare to risk open war by shooting down our planes, once we had made clear that we intended to maintain that airlift and that we were not bluffing.

Second: The United Nations Emergency Forces should be enlarged and strengthened to whatever size events may prove necessary to maintain order until the Suez Canal problem has been completely resolved and a peace treaty between Israel and Egypt has been concluded.

The Suez Canal is the economic jugular vein of the European economy and one of the vital waterways of the world. A stoppage of traffic through the Canal of only a few weeks has paralyzed the European continent and even the Middle East. We have had to ship oil from this country to meet the emergency, although we have been trying to build up our own dwindling oil reserves here to meet future emergencies. I believe very strongly that all the vital waterways of the world, upon which the peace and economy of the world depend, should be freely opened to all commerce. At the Potsdam Conference I tried to get a recognition of this problem of open traffic on the waterways of the world. I urged that the Black Sea Straits, the Kiel Canal, the Rhine and Danube Rivers, the Suez Canal, the Strait of Gibraltar and the Panama Canal be made free waterways for merchant shipping. I suggest that we ought to keep on working to relieve world tensions. And the first practical step we can take along that line is to achieve a permanent settlement of the Suez Canal, for we cannot leave it to the caprices of a military dictator or the political whims of any one nation.

And we must realize that it is naïve and fantastic to hope that we can achieve any kind of peace in the Middle East as long as there are bitterness and open clashes between the Arabs and the Jews. The nation of Israel is here to stay.

The United States, as well as the United Nations, should do everything possible to cool the passions of those extremists who want to destroy Israel. The boundary lines between Israel and Egypt must be settled and those boundaries guaranteed. The United Nations Emergency Forces could play a highly constructive role in this.

Third: In our own interest and in the interest of the peace of the world, we should never again allow ourselves to become separated from our allies. We cannot be part internationalist, part isolationist, part pacifist and part appeasers. We fought two World Wars to keep Britain, France and Western civilization from being destroyed by an ambitious Kaiser and a madman Hitler. At the end of the Second World War we set up a number of important barriers to see that Britain, France and the free world were safe against the threat of international Communism. Vacillation, indecision and failure to state clearly our foreign policy during the past few years and neglecting to keep our allies informed of our aims and intentions contributed to the recent tragic events in the Middle East and almost brought us to a third world war. Perhaps this is no time to remind ourselves that we must assume some responsibility for the panicky military moves of the British, French and Israelis in Egypt. Yet we had better draw a lesson from what happened. I would ask what the American people would think we would do if the Panama Canal were seized in violation of treaties and made subject to the will of a dictator. I know what I would do. I feel certain that if we had kept close diplomatic contact with our allies and maintained a frank and forthright understanding of what was involved in the Middle East, we could well have avoided the debacle that followed. I think it is an historic blunder to have found ourselves on the same side with the expansionist and Communist Russia in a move to rebuke and weaken our allies with whom we had to fight jointly two world wars, because their security and ours are inseparable.

During my Administration we kept an intimate understanding with the leaders of our allies. France and Britain have, for over a century, been with us, and we have managed to get along and cooperate on all major world problems. It was inevitable that, at times, we would find ourselves disagreeing on certain issues, sometimes with Great Britain and sometimes with France. On some occasions we even found ourselves in sharp contention. But we never failed to treat them as free and independent allies. We always got along and worked together for our mutual security and peace. We conducted our relations in a free and candid manner. We never failed to tell each other what we intended to do, and we always did exactly what we said we would do.

As President of the world's leading power, I thought it not only essential but proper to keep the doors of the White House open to all our allies at all times with equal treatment for all. As President, I welcomed the visits of all heads of state, as well as prime ministers and foreign ministers. At the end of the Potsdam Conference, I informed Stalin that if any further joint conferences of heads of government were to be held, they would have to take place in Washington, since President Roosevelt and I had already come to meet them in Europe. Now that we have a promise of a new foreign policy, I hope that all the Allied leaders will soon again be invited to come to Washington and that invitations for such visits will not be limited to a few men we favor or court.

As we back the President in his announced program for the Middle East, let us also make sure that we restore the strength, dignity and prestige of our allies, without whom we cannot be certain of the maintenance of peace for all the people of the world.

———

Before the Bermuda Conference was held in March, 1957, between the President and Prime Minister MacMillan I urged the free world to close ranks to meet resurgent Communist expansionism. This is what I said:

I THINK the time has come for the free nations of the world to close ranks to combat resurgent Russian expansionism in the face of the brutal revival of Stalinism. We need bold and decisive moves to make more effective our grand strategy of common security. Our preoccupation with recent Middle East events has tended to obscure the existence of explosive conditions in other strategic areas of the world.

The more we deal with the Russians, the more we realize that they cannot or will not change their determination to dominate the world. It would be sheer folly for us to assume that we can look to anyone other than our alliance of free nations for our security.

The meeting this week at Bermuda between the President and the British Prime Minister I hope will bring about the restoration of British-American solidarity based on mutual understanding and closer cooperation. It is equally important that we also achieve the fullest understanding and cooperation with the French, and I was glad to see the President take the first step in that direction with Prime Minister Mollet during his recent visit here.

But it is my judgment that the meeting at Bermuda should be followed by consultations with our friends and allies everywhere. We should do this for two reasons: First, we need to restore the machinery of continuous, close consultation so that we do not risk again the dangers of division among us. And second, we need constantly to review and reappraise our methods and measures for dealing with international Communism.

I hate to think how narrow was our escape from disaster in the Middle East when we became separated from our allies. However, we have gained a little more time there, and United Nations emergency forces are on patrol. The Russians have been duly warned. But, as yet, we have solved nothing fundamental, and the threat of war still remains. Until the causes that led to the recent crisis are promptly and wisely dealt with, there will be no peace in the Near East or elsewhere around the world.

The Russian Communists are skilled troublemakers and are ceaselessly engaged in fomenting and exploiting fear and trouble everywhere.

I think we have to be especially vigilant in Germany. The ruthless crushing of Hungary's bid for freedom shows that Russia will not stop at mere intrigue, conspiracy and subversion but will embark on military intervention in cynical disregard of its obligations to the United Nations and world opinion. This points up the danger that exists to the West in similar moves the Kremlin can make at any time it suits its purpose in East Germany.

If the Russians should launch a military operation in East Germany, similar to the one in Hungary, then the security of West Germany and Western Europe will be immediately threatened.

I think there is a second danger zone in Africa. With all Americans, I welcome the statesmanship which brought about the establishment of the independence of Ghana. For Africa, where there are many explosive situations, is a prime target for Russian penetration and exploitation. Russian intrigue with certain political adventurers in Africa is already at work trying to exploit the rising tide of nationalism and growing racial tensions there. Russia is after the vast resources of the African continent for its own benefit.

And there is a third area in which we face immediate and serious trouble—and that is in Southeast Asia and in the Far East, which are in political ferment, and where newly independent nations are being preyed upon by the Communists. There is a grave development in Indonesia where the rich natural resources and remarkable skill and aptitudes of the people have already exposed them to Communist encroachments. The hope of democratic development there is threatened, exposing at the same time the free nations of Australia, New Zealand, the Philippines, and Thailand. For Indonesia is so situated geographically that it could serve as a springboard for intrigue and subversion against this perimeter of free nations by the Communist masters of China and Russia.

In view of these great dangers, I hope the President at Bermuda will henceforth exercise personal leadership in the conduct of our foreign policy. It is impossible, under our system of government, to conduct foreign policy successfully by delegation of the President's personal powers and responsibility. No matter how able the individuals to whom the President may attempt to delegate his powers, it usually leads to confusion and misunderstanding with foreign governments and with our own Congress and people. When I called in Dean Acheson to name him Secretary of State, I said, half seriously, to him: "Dean, you are going to be Secretary of State, but you will not be the President. I have no intention of being my own Secretary of State at any time, but under the Constitution only the President has the power to make foreign policy. I will exercise that power. I expect you to come to me with your recommendations. I will make the final decisions which the Department is to carry out." This policy, faithfully carried out, helped reduce the margin of misunderstanding both with foreign governments, which were kept closely informed, and the Congress, which was always consulted and briefed in strict bipartisanship.

Therefore, beginning with Bermuda, the President has an opportunity to resume personal control which is so essential to restore to the United States its position of world leadership of the free nations.

At Bermuda, I hope the President will undertake to bring Britain back into full partnership for our mutual benefit and security. I cannot subscribe to the contention of some of our experts and self-designated prophets that Britain and

France are in decline and no longer can be depended upon as major powers. These experts would have us abandon historic friendships on the ground that we must now seek out new and rising nations with which we can build more firmly for the future. If I remember my history correctly, the Duke of Wellington and Lord Russell foretold the end of Britain in the 1840's.

This was sheer nonsense in the 1840's. It is sheer nonsense now. The greatness of Britain and France call for no defense from me or anyone else. Their contributions to democracy, industry and science, apart from their culture, are so enormous as to assure their continuance as important factors in civilization for centuries to come. They have come through two terrible wars at enormous sacrifices with their democratic institutions and their cultures standing firm. We should and will do everything in our power to give them encouragement and support, as much for our own sakes as for theirs.

A historic development is now taking place in Europe— the putting into action of an age-long dream of an economically united Europe in which Britain and France would play important roles. Many of the historic trouble spots in Europe would vanish once this dream became a reality.

This would help us to encourage other evolving areas of the world to make use of their resources for their own benefit and the common interest of the peoples of the world.

Let no nation take advantage of the awakening of Asia and Africa for purposes of aggrandizement and exploitation, or set into motion new alignments of power and rivalry. In a world of so much undeveloped resources and riches, there is room and opportunity for all nations to thrive and for all peoples of all colors to achieve their rightful dignity and place among men.

At the Potsdam Conference in 1945, Stalin turned to Churchill in my presence, after the British Prime Minister had made some comment about the Pope, and asked cynically, "How many divisions has the Pope?"

By that one question, Stalin betrayed the crassest ignorance of history, misjudging the real sources of power—the mind and the spirit of men.

Twelve years have passed since Stalin asked this question, and the threat to the free world by the Russians is still with us. History is on the side of the men who believe in the power of the spirit. But until the Russian people do something about their own freedom, we, and the free world, will have to maintain the necessary divisions. That is the only condition the Communist rulers appear to respect.

―――――――――

When in October, 1957, the launching of the Sputnik by Russia shook the confidence of the free world in American leadership, and Khrushchev began to assume a truculent attitude, I urged the government to meet the Russian challenge as follows:

IF we are to meet the current Russian challenge, I would urge the immediate setting up of a new government agency headed by a strong and able man, responsible only to the President, to be in absolute charge of our long-range missiles.

I would suggest further that Congress be asked to amend the McMahon Act to make possible the pooling and exchange of scientific research with our British ally, now forbidden by this act.

And I think we ought to put an end to our unilateral disarmament, still going on, and reassess our military budget and requirements. The time for "business as usual" is over. The launching of the Russian earth satellite has shaken some of the confidence of the free world in our ability to maintain leadership. The sooner we repair this damage, the more certain will be the security of free nations everywhere.

Let there be no misunderstanding, for unless we are strong, peace will be in jeopardy. And Russian propaganda may even now deceive some nations into misjudging our real power and potential and panic some people into surrender and compromise, as some were bullied by Hitler into doing.

Khrushchev's truculence today should serve as a warning to us of what the Soviets really would be tempted to do if they had a preponderance of power, and our principal concern is to be ever vigilant that they never gain that preponderance. Even a temporary technical advance with Sputnik has been seized by the Russians as an opportunity to accelerate the Cold War with brazen threats and bold-faced lies. It would be dangerous for us, however, to underrate the scientific achievement of Sputnik and its confirmation that the Russians possess the means to launch long-range missiles.

This is not the first time this country has fallen behind

a nation with aggressive designs concentrating all of its resources on production for conquest. But once aroused, invariably we have overtaken and swiftly surpassed such aggressors. Arrogant dictators never seem to learn the capacity of the American people to rise to a challenge once their freedom is threatened. Khrushchev is today repeating that historic mistake of underestimating and misjudging the spirit and capacity of the American people and other free nations. The Communist boss of Russia, is, in fact, doing us a service in his efforts to frighten us.

But let us not shut our eyes to the fact that we did let down our guard. The consequence of our mistake could be grave, indeed, unless we quickly remedy the situation. Our survival may be at stake.

No longer can we risk a single moment of complacency, nor the beguiling of our citizens with a false sense of security through pronouncements instead of action, nor can we afford dereliction of duty, passing of the buck and interservice rivalry and bickering.

Our immediate task is to bring into production the long-range missile. And we must hasten the launching of an earth satellite. An earth satellite, for our peaceful purposes, would aid scientists the world over to learn more of the shape and the secrets of the space around us. But let us beware of the prospect that, in evil hands, an earth satellite might be employed as a weapon of war. Some of the Soviet propaganda is already hinting at such a prospect.

But we are not going to produce long-range missiles by divided authority in any of the existing departments. I found that out during my Administration. As soon as I saw that the program was lagging due to interservice rivalry, I called in one of the top production engineering men of industry and one of the most highly respected in the nation. I placed him in full charge of the missile program responsible only to the President and with instructions to knock heads together wherever it was necessary to break through bottlenecks. And I assured him that I would back him to the hilt.

By 1952 this program had made encouraging progress, but with the change of administration, the head of this operation was one of the first to be dismissed, although he was of the same political affiliation as the new administration. I can only assume that the reason for his dismissal was the fact that he had been appointed by another President.

What happened in the ensuing years represents a sorry chapter in the story of our defense. I wonder what our position would be today if we had followed an irresolute and divided and partisan course when we undertook to harness atomic energy and produce an atomic bomb, when we later launched a crash program to develop the hydrogen bomb, and when we undertook to produce the first nuclear submarine. We would have lost precious time, and we would have run the risk of losing the race, first to the Germans and then to the Soviets.

But whatever mistakes we have made, time, in my judgment, is as yet on our side, providing we take immediate action. Neither panic nor recriminations will avail us anything. What could be bad would be Russia's succeeding in coming between us and our allies in her grand strategy of divide and conquer. This is why I welcome the resumption of closer collaboration between Great Britain and the United States. I think part of our difficulties in foreign affairs has developed from our failure to understand and cooperate with our friends and allies in vitally strategic areas. The coming of Prime Minister MacMillan to the United States for the purpose, among other things, of bringing about the pooling of scientific knowledge and facilities between our two nations will go a long way to strengthen our defense efforts against Communist imperialism.

I am hopeful that Congress will see the wisdom and the need of agreeing to amend the McMahon Act so that the President may be empowered to exchange information with the British. Lest we forget, the British initiated the atomic bomb project and then turned it over to us, thereby helping it immeasurably to an earlier success.

It was natural for us to want to safeguard the secrets of the atomic bomb, since it was an awesome weapon and a major deterrent against any new despotic military aggressor.

The McMahon Act was the statutory expression of the American mood at that time to retain sole custody of the atomic bomb secrets in the United States. Since Britain had been a partner with us in the initiation of the atomic bomb and a close ally during two world wars, I, for one, felt that Canada and Great Britain should be allowed a closer association with us in this field. But for all practical purposes at that time, Canada and Britain were in no economic position to manufacture the bomb. Both had reason to expect that American possession of the bomb would safeguard their security as well as our own.

In the course of time, the McMahon Act served to prevent us from having the benefit of the latest research of Britain and Canada, and Britain felt compelled on her own to duplicate at great hardship the construction of and experiments with nuclear bombs. I think the time has come to stop fooling ourselves that we know all the answers or can forever maintain a monopoly of any scientific development. Therefore, within reasonable safeguards our security would be served best by cooperating in a two-way exchange of information between the British and us.

Our next important task is to take a hard and realistic look at our total national budget, and with particular attention to defense.

In my judgment, the defense budget should be determined by the realities of the world conflict we are in, rather than primarily on the basis of our understandable and proper desire to reduce expenses. Our appropriations for defense—without waste and certainly without duplication—must be based on the grave requirements of our security and not on the premise that we are living in a normal world at peace and that we can afford to relax. We should fit our budget to our defense needs and not our defense needs to our budget.

The Sputnik has reminded us again that we are confronted by a resourceful and powerful adversary. We ought not to be taken in by frequent attempts of the Soviets to throw us off balance by talks of peaceful coexistence when we see that every move they make is calculated to achieve world domination.

The one indomitable obstacle to their ambition is the military, economic and political strength of the United States and her free allies. That is why we need to give security priority over our comforts, thus seeking to balance the budget through personal sacrifices rather than by national weakness. The resources of our nation are immense, and our people, like all free, determined people, will meet challenges that enslaved people under dictatorships never do.

I would suggest that the Administration undertake a sweeping reappraisal of its military requirements and pay due regard to our growing need for scientific research and personnel. We need not only to attract our best scientific minds but also to encourage our best students to higher education and devotion to pure science on which our modern world depends.

If this nation gets the proper kind of leadership, it will make all the sacrifices required of it to meet the new challenge to peace as it always has in the past.

In January, 1958, I urged that Russian leaders be given every opportunity to prove their peaceful intentions. I wrote, in part, the following:

I BELIEVE Premier Bulganin of Soviet Russia and Communist Boss Khrushchev ought to get every opportunity to prove they really want peace.

Khrushchev may be making a virtue of necessity since the maintenance of the still very large conventional Russian ground forces is a serious drain upon the labor supply of the Soviet economy. The Soviet Union labor supply is beginning to feel the pinch caused by the low birth rates and high infant mortality of 1941-1945.

I have had some experience with the makers of Kremlin policy. From my first day as President, when I told Molotov that peace was a two-way street and that Russia would have to make her contribution by backing her words with deeds, I have had reason to have little faith in the promises of Communist leaders.

Their present aim is to intimidate and frighten into acceptance of their terms those peoples and nations they cannot control for their own imperialistic purposes. And it is dangerous business to appease dictators who boast of their ability through modern science to annihilate those who would oppose them while professing at the same time to seek peace and international accord.

The Soviet Union has hitherto refused to cooperate with the free nations on real disarmament or control of arms and has used every conference or international discussion on disarmament merely to further her own design for conquest. In the face of past failures and even realizing the Russians still are seeking only further grist for their peace propaganda mills, while they arm for imperialistic purposes, we ought to put the burden of proof on the Russians by answering them with a concrete counter-proposal.

The American reply to Premier Bulganin and Communist Boss Khrushchev should be an invitation to start immediate talks through diplomatic channels—between Washington and Moscow—seeking to arrive at some minimum yet verifiable and practicable agreement on armed forces or weapons.

If a basis for even such a minimum accord is possible through negotiations through diplomatic channels—and through diplomatic channels only—then Bulganin and Khrushchev might be reminded that three Presidents of the United States traveled thousands of miles to meet with Russian leaders. The Russians now in their turn must travel to the New World to prove their sincerity.

A proper meeting place for the Russians to sign an accord already agreed upon through diplomatic channels could be Washington, or in New York, where the United Nations was organized.

But we should meet with the Russians only if our friends and allies of NATO are in full agreement with us that the Russians are making a concrete and useful step towards peace and control of arms. We must never make the mistake again of not consulting our allies at all times.

There can be no serious objections to the Russians raising any questions—military, political or economic, provided they are raised through diplomatic channels and not through phony peace propaganda speeches or letters or attacks on this country or our allies.

The door ought to be left wide open for the fullest and frankest exchange through diplomatic channels.

But there must be no secret agreements. And there must be no doubt in the minds of the Kremlin leaders that we intend to take any and all measures to keep our armed strength powerful enough to maintain our security and freedom and that of our allies until the Soviets abandon their program of world conquest.

We therefore need prompt and vigorous steps to fill in the serious gaps in our defense requirements.

The most important thing is to coordinate the missiles

program. Someone with authority to compel the armed services to agree to a program should be appointed. Only such a "boss," able to appeal directly to the President and having the President's absolute support, can meet our badly lagging missile needs and those of our allies.

But missiles alone are not a total basis for a defense program. All branches of our armed forces must be maintained at a high state of efficiency to meet any emergency. It would be a mistake to depend upon any single weapon or any single service to meet any challenge whether by conventional or new-type weapons. We must have a strong army, a strong navy and a hard-hitting air force.

And what we should be prepared to meet is the dangerous threat of the Russian submarine fleet, greater than any submarine fleet in history.

We already have the beginnings of a powerful nuclear fleet and nuclear submarines that ought to be constructed in greater numbers. The cruising range of these submarines submerged is fantastic and they constitute launching platforms elusive to the enemy.

Until we can get some workable agreement on arms limitation, we must face frankly the tremendous cost of modern defense.

We believe in economy, and a balanced budget. Therefore, a tax levy should be made to meet the increasing costs of essential security. And the sooner we face up to the need for such a tax, the sooner we will avoid piling up a federal debt that might become unmanageable.

The American people will understand the need for such a tax if it is put up to them frankly.

The American people are always ready to follow a

leader, but not blindly. They must know where he is going and that he speaks the truth.

———————

In April, 1959, with the appointment of Christian A. Herter as the new Secretary of State and the projected visit of the Vice President to Russia, I suggested that if Soviet Premier Khrushchev indicated any interest to come to the United States it might be well to encourage him. I said:

IF the forthcoming visit of the Vice President to Moscow can help in some way, and if it provides the Kremlin with an opportunity to clear some of the air, then I am all for it. The Vice President not only will carry with him the prestige of his office, but will go as a special instrument of the President.

Should Premier Khrushchev indicate that he, himself, would like to visit Washington, it might be well to encourage him. I think Khrushchev needs first-hand exposure to the United States and a good look at it to balance off his over-assessment of what his missiles and industrial might can do to frighten us.

I tried to persuade Stalin to visit the United States on several occasions, but I was led to understand that he could not risk the trip because of the situation at home.

But after my own trip to Potsdam and the previous trips of Roosevelt to meet Stalin, I felt that there was no longer any sense for an American President to meet the Russian dictators at their convenience and thought it was high time they came to meet with us here.

We traveled great distances to show that even as a leading power we did not insist upon anyone coming to see us on our own grounds. Dictators have a way of summoning spokesmen of other nations either to bully or beguile them into surrender or false security.

Moscow, as the capital of the Communist world, has staged meetings of satellites, neighbors and so-called neutrals intended to propagandize the notion that all roads lead to Moscow.

From time to time some members of the Kremlin have traveled to Peiping to placate the Red Chinese dictators, in recognition of that country's rapidly developing power and its position as a possible rival. But the seat of the Communist and satellite world continues to be physically in Moscow and in the Kremlin.

In June, I again urged that Khrushchev come to the United States, saying in part as follows:

I THINK the sooner Khrushchev comes to Washington—as I hear he wants to—the sooner we might clear the air and get down to a realistic approach on the critical issues that plague the world.

There are some who believe everything could be settled if only Khrushchev sat down with the President of the United States in a man-to-man talk.

These are people who obviously have had no experience in dealing with Soviet Russia or have short memories of the long list of Soviet betrayals and failures to keep commitments.

I believe, nevertheless, that no door should be closed even to the remotest chance in pursuit of peace.

We must not give the Communist propagandists any opportunities to raise false hopes about their peaceful intentions by exploiting any failure of Khrushchev's realizing his wish to come here.

I do not see why anyone should be afraid to have Khrushchev come here at this time. Let Khrushchev see for himself what we are and how determined we are, as a people, to retain our freedom and resist any attempt to separate us from any of our allies and the free world. And when it comes to blandishments and the new grin, he will see that we are all from Missouri and have to be shown.

If Khrushchev means business and genuinely wants peace, he will find the nations of the free world always ready to act and act swiftly.

Khrushchev will see here what Mikoyan saw—that the resoluteness of the United States to remain free and the might of the United States to back up its determination to be free leaves no room for appeasement or expedient compromise at the expense of any people anywhere. But this resoluteness must not be misunderstood by the Communist world as the type of intransigence which the Russians have adopted as their practice in their program for world domination.

We have never sought to dominate the world, or exploit any people, or force our will or our system of government on any nation, firm and dedicated as we are in our democratic institutions. Russian intransigence and their abuse of their membership in the United Nations has made it almost impossible to discuss any issue with them on a plane of reason and in an atmosphere of quiet and understanding.

Because of this and the Communists' persistent plotting and trouble-making around the world, we have been forced to look to our strength, military and economic, as the only practical recourse to protect our freedom and our security.

And that is why we have had to make great sacrifices and set aside vast portions of our resources to help keep other nations of the free world free. And Khrushchev should remember that we will never falter nor tire—no matter what the cost nor how long it may take—in our efforts to remain free.

Unless Khrushchev understands the eternal desire of the American people to resist tyranny, his visit here would be futile. If Khrushchev continues to delude himself that the Kremlin can, by either keeping up the Cold War or threatening us in Berlin, or anywhere else, get us to weaken, then his visit should be an opportunity for the President to set him straight, face to face.

I think this Washington meeting would help to put a little more spine into some of the politically ambitious and confused men among us and our allies who compound our difficulties. I am sure that our allies should have no valid ground for any misgivings that such a talk in Washington would lead to anything of any nature that was not in full conformity with our intention never again to separate from our allies. On that score of keeping at work with our allies of the free world in unity of purpose and in concert, we are a determined and a united people.

In October, 1959, commenting on the Khrushchev disarmament proposals, I said the time had come for the Communists to prove their sincerity:

THE Communist world is now being informed by Nikita Khrushchev that the American government and the American people do not want war.

I hope that the results of this declared change of attitude toward this country will serve the interests of peace.

I would urge that we be alert to developments in the trouble spots of Europe and Asia to make certain that we are not led to misjudge the true facts or permit the Communists to misunderstand exactly what we are prepared to do.

These troubled areas where peace and freedom have been threatened or are in jeopardy have not been of our making, and it is there that we will look for the first proof of the avowed renunciation of the use of force in international dealings or interference in the internal affairs of other nations.

Never in history has the need for disarmament been so imperative and so intimately involved in the everyday life of our people.

While he was here, Khrushchev made certain suggestions as part of a sweeping Utopian disarmament program. Some of those suggestions are realistic where they deal with supervised controls in a gradual process of reducing arms stage by stage.

These suggestions could be an important contribution if Khrushchev follows through with concrete proposals and commitments which he will keep.

There can be no realistic disarmament without adequate supervision and control by the United Nations. I would remind Chairman Khrushchev that when we had the monopoly of nuclear weapons we offered to place them under international supervision.

But Stalin and the Kremlin rejected our proposal, because they would not agree to control and inspection. If Khrushchev and the Kremlin now are ready to reconsider the need for control and inspection, they can make a constructive step to ease the burden of armaments.

The United States in this century has taken the lead on several occasions in an effort to bring about disarmament, only to meet disappointment and disillusion.

And when we did make drastic reductions, either because of agreement by treaty, as in the case of the London Naval Agreement, or because of national policy of strengthening civilian economy, we found ourselves confronted by grave danger to our security as a nation.

This time, let us make sure that we do not endanger our strength and security by making disproportionate sacrifices or by being lured into a false peace.

I am glad that the President has postponed his planned visit to Moscow and Russia, whatever the stated reason for the change. More time is needed to see whether Khrushchev will follow his words with deeds.

In previous meetings with President Roosevelt, myself and President Eisenhower, the Soviet leaders entered into solemn agreements and commitments which could have led to world cooperation for peace, but which have been breached or ignored. This is how the Cold War started and how it continued. We tried everything we could to prevent this Cold War.

Only Khrushchev and the Kremlin can put an end to the Cold War. Only they can bring the thaw. Khrushchev said it would take time to work out changes. One of the first things he might do while in Peiping is to bring about a change in Red China's approach to international conduct. I hope there is some substance to the dispatches from Red China that Khrushchev is urging Mao Tse-tung to adopt a course of caution and moderation. And on Khrushchev's return to Moscow, let us see what he does to ease the tensions.

Despite the experience and rebuffs we have had in our past efforts to get the Soviet Union to cooperate, our people would give united support to the President in dealing with any constructive proposals by Moscow.

I still do not think it advisable for the President to go to Moscow. Long before the Vice President went there, I favored and suggested that Khrushchev be invited to this country. I did this because I believed he ought to learn first-hand from the President in the White House where we stood, as a united people, on the issues which divide us from the Kremlin. I thought it was about time that the head of the Soviet Union should call on the President here, since three Presidents had traveled overseas to meet with the leaders of the Soviet Union.

But there is a deeper implication to consider in the President's visit to Moscow. Lest we forget, we are dealing with a ruthless dictatorship which has imposed its will over millions of people. Need we be reminded again of the fate of the people of Poland and Hungary, Rumania and Bulgaria, where Stalin had agreed with Churchill and Attlee and me to hold free elections? There are other Communist-subjugated peoples in Europe and elsewhere. What about these people? Until Khrushchev shows some kind of good faith in repudiating Stalinism by living up to the agreements made with us at Yalta and Potsdam, I would hope that a President of the United States would not lend himself and the prestige of his office to the appearance of supporting the Kremlin policy by going personally to Moscow.

I think it was all right for the Vice President to go, and I think there should be no hesitancy in sending any other high-ranking representative of the President to keep discussions and negotiations going, in concert with our allies.

As long as we are alert, the longer we talk, the better our chances will be of avoiding a third world war. And the longer we talk, the better the chances are of not rushing into ill-considered compromises or sacrificing the rights of other people.

Time is on our side if we know what we are doing and where we are going. Time is always on the side of free people. No government of the United States has ever refused or will ever refuse to discuss the issues confronting the world with any power, large or small. We believe in justice and freedom and a good life for everyone and no interference in the internal affairs of anyone. We do not seek to impose our way of life or system of government on any nation, and Russia is welcome to her Communism.

We fear no competition from her politically, industrially or economically.

But we will resist all attempts at subversion, direct or indirect. Whatever claims Chairman Khrushchev made to his American audiences about people choosing Communism and having political freedom to do so, the undeniable fact remains that no nation has ever adopted Communism voluntarily. And no Communist-imposed government has ever dared to face a free election where the people had a fair choice of government.

I hope that the private talks between President Eisenhower and Chairman Khrushchev at Camp David were useful. Time will tell. On the surface, some of our people seem to have impressed Khrushchev, and Khrushchev seems to have impressed some of our people.

It is interesting to note that Khrushchev seemed to be more comfortable with our big businessmen and our financiers than he was with our top labor leaders. Many of our labor leaders have been to Russia and were unjustly accused by some of our big businessmen of being soft on Communism. But it turns out that most of these labor leaders saw enough for themselves to realize that Russian Communism was no good for free labor, either economically or politically.

Khrushchev has proved himself to be a very expert

propagandist and dynamic advocate of his ideology. But his arrogant nonsense, when referring to this country as a pure capitalist society, in that Marxian jargon of his, may confuse for a time some of the underdeveloped countries of the world. But it really should fool no one. As a matter of fact, Russia is the capitalist nation—with a small, all-powerful clique in control of all the wealth and resources. The Communists say the people own everything—but in reality they own nothing and live under state capitalism with no competition, and no accounting from their bosses.

Ours is, in all essential respects, a free competitive enterprise society, the basis of which is the freedom and the supremacy of the individual.

Chairman Khrushchev made the most of his opportunities and access to our radio, television and press to expound his Communist views to the American people. He took considerable license with the facts.

In November, 1959, I raised the question about our self-imposed ban on nuclear tests, which created some controversy. But subsequent events proved what I had to say not altogether unfounded. I wrote:

I DO not think it makes any sense to continue our self-imposed ban on all nuclear tests, and we ought to lift it immediately.

Let us stop deluding ourselves with the hope that this sacrifice will persuade the Kremlin to agree to foolproof international nuclear control and disarmament. If we allow ourselves to drift into a position where we fall behind in scientific nuclear development, we will compromise our security and possibly jeopardize the peace.

I do not like to think of nuclear testing in terms of military application only and, of course, I would prefer that we concentrate all of our efforts on the peaceful development of the greatest potential source of energy so far discovered by man. But as long as there is open international lawlessness in the making of weapons, then we have an obligation to keep ourselves militarily strong.

Scientists have found that important nuclear tests can now be staged and controlled underground with all the fall-out sealed in. Whatever risks of further contamination of the atmosphere from fall-out there may be from tests in the open, there seems to be no longer any valid reasons for stopping experiments underground.

I am informed by scientists that underground nuclear explosions are not always detectable and may be mistaken for earthquakes. That is all the more reason why we should not handicap ourselves unilaterially at this time. We have to have more verifiable assurances than mere declarations by the Communists of what they are doing and what they intend to do.

This is why we ought to resume making underground tests without any further delay.

I regard as a constructive approach to international co-operation the recent suggestion of British Foreign Secretary

Selwyn Lloyd that the United States, Britain and the Soviet Union hold a joint series of underground nuclear tests.

I do not see why France ought not be invited to take part in such joint ventures. From all indications, France is about to take her place as a nuclear power and I think that this is all to the good. I, for one, am glad to see that a nation that has been for so long so valiant a champion of freedom can become a stronger ally for peace. We ought to be pleased that France is reaping the fruits of the invaluable contributions her scientists have made to nuclear research.

We would all be pleasantly surprised if the Soviet Union ever accepted such a proposal as that made by Mr. Lloyd. But I see no reason why our policy should be decided on assumptions or expectations of what the Soviet Union will eventually agree to do. Let us not be lulled into holding up our own progress at this critical phase of international trends.

I cannot easily forget that we lost a decade in which we might have concentrated entirely on the peaceful use of the atom instead of diverting the creative efforts of men to the making of terrible weapons.

The Soviet Union is responsible for this lost decade. Because, at a time when we had the exclusive possession of the atomic weapon, I thought that in keeping with the needs of mankind, the United States should propose to internationalize control and possession of nuclear production.

And we did offer officially to place the means of production of atomic devices within the jurisdiction of the United Nations for the benefit of all peoples. Under this proposal the making of atomic weapons would have stopped and the world could have devoted its energies to the peaceful development of the atom.

I keep bringing up these facts from time to time to remind some statesmen and those people who are now so alarmed about the danger of fall-out that none of this would be disturbing us if the Soviet Union had not brutally rejected this extraordinary offer by the one government which had complete control at the time. In history there is no precedent for that action.

We of the United States who had the bomb, the know-how and the facilities were willing to submit to the necessary international inspection. But the Kremlin, intent on its program of world domination, would not agree to inspection and thus vetoed and destroyed a great opportunity for international cooperation and peace.

Thus today, since other nations are in a position to make nuclear tests at will, we have no choice but to continue our experiments. Let us not be maneuvered into a false position by propaganda that attempts to picture us as a weapon-conscious and military-minded people. There is no need to appease these false accusers by depriving ourselves of the necessary and continuing experiments in the nuclear field so that we can expand our knowledge.

You can never freeze any discovery. You must go on experimenting. There can be no improvement without continuous experiments and tests. We know that from what we see and have today in our everyday life. It was not too long ago that Edison produced the first electric light bulb and the phonograph and a great many of us still remember the first automobile. And look at what we have already achieved in the field of nuclear science. And we must never discourage the pursuit of pure science in its quest for knowledge.

The problems of expanding, harnessing and controlling nuclear energy pose vast difficulties and entail certain dangers. But how are we going to get the answers to many questions unless we allow our scientists full sway to experiment and explore?

And now that we can continue such experiments underground without damage to the atmosphere, we should get on with it. I hope that in the future we can do this cooperatively with other nations.

I have been questioned about a recently published statement quoting General Marshall to the effect that at the time of the bombing of Hiroshima and Nagasaki we used the only two atomic bombs in our possession and that we had no others in reserve.

I feel that General Marshall may have been misunderstood or he may have wished to withhold further information at the time he was questioned.

For years I have urged General Marshall to set down in his own words the story of his life and the many great contributions he made to the nation and the world.

Had he written his own full account, I think he would undoubtedly have recorded that the manufacture of additional A-bombs was continuing at the same rate at which the first two had been produced after the original atomic explosion took place at Alamagordo, New Mexico, on the sixteenth of July, 1945. The bomb over Hiroshima exploded August 6 and the one over Nagasaki, August 9.

There were other A-bombs in the course of production in varying stages of completion awaiting only the results of how the first bombs worked. And we soon had a substantial reserve of A-bombs in our stockpile.

I have also been asked whether it would be possible for any nuclear bomb to be set off as a result of false alarm that the enemy had attacked us, or by some irresponsible person.

I can make the categorical statement that no nuclear bomb can be triggered by any one person regardless of rank without the expressed and personal order of the President of the United States.

No one person is ever in a position to put together a nuclear bomb to be ready for action without involving a group of men who are required for this purpose. The precautions taken are fully adequate against any rash act.

I cannot, of course, be sure of the circumstances surrounding the steps necessary to be taken under a totalitarian government. If some dictator should become involved in circumstances which might threaten his personal rule, there is no way of knowing whether or not he might not in a mad moment resort to a nuclear bomb.

We would all feel a lot better if there were some assurances that the world would never be subjected to such a madness. That is why we ought to control internationally all such weapons to assure the nations that no rash act by a power-mad dictator could plunge the world into disaster.

AUTHOR'S NOTE

SOME TIME back in May, 1959, I went to the Walter Reed Hospital to call on General George C. Marshall. It was the last time I saw him. When I came out of his room, I was informed that Secretary of State John Foster Dulles was on the same floor. I walked down the hallway and met the Secretary of State as he came in from a period in the sun outside the hospital. Then he told me that he had been very happy that, in the articles I had written for the North American Newspaper Alliance, I had supported the foreign policy of the United States. I told him that I thought all good citizens should support the basic American foreign policy and that only the President can act on foreign policy as the Constitution provides.

–H.S.T.

02072